# The Summer Camp Memory Book

# The Summer Camp Memory Book

### A Pictorial Treasury of Everything
### —from Campfires to Color Wars—
### You Loved about Camp

*Richard J. S. Gutman* and *Kellie O. Gutman*

CROWN PUBLISHERS, INC.     NEW YORK

*For Pop, Mandy, and Bobby*

ALSO BY THE AUTHORS

*John Wilkes Booth Himself*

*American Diner,* with Elliott Kaufman
  and David Slovic

Published by Crown Publishers, Inc.,
One Park Avenue, New York, New York 10016
and simultaneously in Canada by General Publishing Company Limited
Manufactured in the United States of America
Library of Congress Cataloging in Publication Data
Gutman, Richard.
The summer camp memory book.
1. Camps—United States—Miscellanea.   I. Gutman,
Kellie O.   II. Title.
GV193.G87 1983      796.54′2′0973      83-7807
ISBN 0-517-54743-0
Book design by Camilla Filancia based on page layouts
by Richard J. S. Gutman and Kellie O. Gutman
10 9 8 7 6 5 4 3 2 1
First Edition

# Contents

ACKNOWLEDGMENTS    vii

INTRODUCTION    1

CHOOSING THE CAMP    3

NAME TAPES    7

GETTING THERE    13

BEHOLD THE CAMP    21

LIVING WITH KIDS    27

RISE AND SHINE    33

FIELDS, DIAMONDS, AND COURTS    37

INDIAN LORE    41

LET NATURE TAKE ITS COURSE    45

BUDDY UP!    51

SPORTS THAT SAY "CAMP"    57

SADDLED UP    61

MEALTIME    65

REST HOUR    69

ARTS AND CRAFTS    75

BEYOND SWIMMING    79

DAY TRIPS    85

CAMPCRAFT    91

TO YOUR HEALTH    95

BEHIND THE FOOTLIGHTS    97

OVERNIGHTS    103

RAINY DAY     111

SPECIAL EVENTS     113

VISITOR'S DAY     117

USUALLY ON SUNDAY     119

CAMPFIRE     121

AFTER DARK     125

COLOR WAR!     133

TRADITIONS     139

END OF THE SEASON     143

PHOTOGRAPH CREDITS     149

# Acknowledgments

It's hard to do an illustrated book without the generous help of many people. We were fortunate to be given free rein in the archives of many camps and campers, who graciously loaned us materials for the research and production of this book. It literally could not have been completed without their help. First and foremost we would like to thank:

Roy C. Ballentine, Kehonka; Joan Bogart, Wicosuta; Max Caldwell, Kennolyn; Donald S. Cheley, Cheley Colorado Camps; Betty Cobb, Runoia; Helen Herz Cohen, Walden; Rosalie P. Corson, Interlochen Center for the Arts; Tim Ellis, Chewonki; Marsha Elmore, Waldemar; Bill Freeman, Andover-Waldron; Katherine Gulick Fricker, Luther Gulick Camps; John Harvey, Yawgoog; Stanley Hirsch, Androscoggin; Sheldon Hoch, Watitoh; Richard Krasker, Forest Acres, Indian Acres; Joe Kruger, Mah-Kee-Nac; Dorothy Langer, Lenore-Owaissa; Bernie Lemonick, Kennebec; Bert Margolis, Greylock; Jean McMullan, Alford Lake; Harry Meyers, Kennebec; Monroe Moss, Lenox for Boys; Jon Myers, Tripp Lake; Saul Nechtem, Bauercrest; Ron Nelson, Ocoee; Alan Ordway, Winona; Sarah Priestman, Unalayee; Tom Reed, Pemigewassett; Mike and Lenore Rogers, Tapawingo; William J. Schmidt, Dudley; Bob Spencer, Greater Boston YMCA; Bobby Strauss, Wigwam; George Sudduth, Wyonegonic; Louise Gulick Van Winkle, Luther Gulick Camps.

Not all camps had photo collections intact or at hand. But the visits were just as pleasant, and we appreciate their spokespeople taking the time to talk to us and show us around:

William Berndt, O-At-Ka; Allen Cramer, Somerset; Alan B. Douglas, Lawrence; Anne Fritz, Arcadia; Mort Goldman, Takajo; Louise Henderson, Arcadia; Malcolm J. Itkin, Kohut; Marjorie Douglas Jefferson, Douglas Ranch Camps; Maxine King, Fernwood; Bob and Phil Lilienthal, Winnebago; Dave Mason, Agawam; Don Shellenberger, Becket; Esta Snider, Pembroke; Nathan Todaro, North Woods.

A number of people shared their time, memories, writings and mementos with us. We would like to thank them all:

Bill Alterman; Armand Ball, executive vice-president, American Camping Association; Charles and Jane Baum; Carole and David Berkowitz; Dr. Eliot Berson; Ronald Blau; Steve Catalano; Jane Cecere; Jennifer Cecere; Robert Jordan Dingley, Naples Historical Society; Leslie Evans; Evan Feigenbaum; Linda Fugate; Susan M. Ginns; Kenneth Greif; Hank and Anne Gutman; I. Cyrus and Mildred Gutman; Lisa Kabnick; Leonard Katowitz;

Hank Ketcham, for permission to reproduce the Dennis the Menace comic strip; Dr. Steve Kruskall; Hope and Norman Makransky; Chuck Miller, for his wonderful book, *A Catawba Assembly*; Harriet Moss; Fern and Charles Nesson; Teresa Phinny, New England Camping Association; David Prendergast; Dr. Paul Rosenberg; Renie Kay Seff; Tom Shapiro; Lynn Sheren; Peggy Sheren; Lynne Spiegel; Candy Stoumen; Hildy Stoumen; Virginia and Donald Trescott; Vassar Book Sale, Washington, D.C.; H. Arnold Wilder, Boston and Maine Railroad Historical Society; Frank and Virginia Williams.

Of course, there were many other campers and counselors, former and present-day, who expressed their opinions on a book about camp. We were glad to hear their thoughts.

Last, we'd like to thank our team at Crown: David Groff, our tireless editorial assistant, and our two editors, Nach Waxman and Barbara Grossman . . . both of whom went to camp and, luckily, liked it.

# The Summer Camp Memory Book

*What better way to spend time waiting for swim period than reading a book in the shade of a spotless tent on a hot summer day?*

One moonlit evening in late August, while we sat around the dying embers of the campfire at Camp Wigwam in Maine, the idea for this book was born. The occasion was the Third Annual Camper-Parent Week, when former campers and their families, as well as parents of present-day campers, came to spend five glorious days on the shores of Bear Lake doing all those things that campers do.

It was, perhaps, not a typical vacation—but then it was not a typical group of people. The men were from many walks of life but had one thing in common: camp. Their memories of those days long ago were so strong and so good that they were worth trying to relive.

While the days were spent in a frenzy of activities, the nights were filled with stories of camp: the old legends, the classic pranks, the closest color wars. It didn't matter to the alumni that they hadn't all been at camp at the same time. In fact, that made it easier to identify more nameless faces in the countless panoramic camp photographs adorning the lodge.

A large part of one evening was devoted to determining the ten most eccentric characters in the history of the camp; nominations had to be supported with actual incidents of bizarre and/or outlandish behavior. Later, a great to-do was made over a photo of four left-handed tennis players. Was it a fake? Was the photo reversed? The issue was somewhat resolved when one former camper stepped forward, identified all four, and vouched for at least three being genuine lefties.

Given the flood of memories brought forth at the reunion, it seemed like a good idea to gather together in a book some mementos and adventures of camp to jog the memories of former campers from any camp.

It is the experience of spending the summer at camp that we have tried to capture. The book is not set in any one particular era but delves into camp life throughout its history. The material we used was as varied as the camp day: precious snapshots from personal scrapbooks; letters to and from campers; posed, formal photographs from camps we could visit; camp brochures and song books; and, of course, camper publications—camp from the campers' viewpoints. These, as much as the text, tell the story of a season at camp.

*Camp "big brothers" could always be conned into a ride— at least part of the way—to the lodge.*

1

*A clear, spring-fed mountain lake is a good drawing card for any camp. And who wouldn't be impressed with that multitude of counselors keeping an eye on the youngsters?*

# Choosing the Camp

How did you first learn you were going to camp? It may have been doctor's orders: At the suggestion of your allergist, a pollen-free summer was called for. Or perhaps it was a family tradition: Your parents had been campers, your older brother and sister had been going for years, and at last you had reached that magical age. Another time-honored rationale was that all your friends went to camp, and there would be no one home in the summer with whom you could play. (A justification employed by parents and children alike.)

Whether it was mutually agreed upon or a decision unilaterally handed down by your parents—"You are *going* to camp this summer"—the next step in the process was to choose the camp. Even though there are more than 10,000 camps in the United States to choose from, probably 9,992 were instantly ruled out. After all, how many brochures would you want to send away for and then try to read? The most important source of information, and probably the most reliable, was word of mouth—the camp's reputation.

No matter how you narrowed down the field, it was *de rigueur* to meet the directors during the winter. If you were lucky they came directly to your house. Otherwise you had to travel to a distant metropolis to have your interview in a stuffy hotel room. The whole affair was akin to a college interview, watered down to the level of a ten-year-old.

When the director came to your house he was armed with anything from an old scrapbook and a new brochure to a tray of slides or a film. A person of uncommon friendliness and good nature, the camp director was a walking, talking brochure, full of rousing good stories about days at camp, humorous asides ("Boys will be boys"), and earnest pronouncements on the joys and benefits of summer camp.

The first time you saw a director's presentation it was pretty exciting. By the time the third or fourth one rolled around it was all beginning to sound familiar—the pat phrases and the little jokes about camp pranks. It wasn't that you questioned the director's veracity, but the food couldn't really be *that* good. All in all it was a classic sales pitch that somehow had to appeal to a ten-year-old and his or her parents at the same time.

You were being interviewed as much as your parents were interviewing the director. You had to measure up to those gung-ho campers of whom you had just seen pictures. An early brochure for Marienfeld Camp in New Hampshire, announcing its sixth season in 1901, stated their entrance requirements:

### WHAT A PARENT SHOULD EXPECT

If the boy or girl has been deprived of electric lights and modern plumbing during the year, perhaps these would be the most desirable things to seek in a camp. If surfeited with the gadgets of civilization and capable of appreciating the hardships of the primitive life, then he or she should have opportunity to sleep on a growth of spruce bed, to know the light of the camp-fire as the only night illumination.

*From Porter Sargent's* A Handbook of Summer Camps, *1934 edition.*

### WINONA
#### A Camp for Boys

The joy and zest of the great outdoors is the heritage of Winona campers. Lakes and rivers, woods and mountains challenge exploration. A swift canter on wilderness roads, a splash in the glowing lake, a sail on the rippling water, a glorious battle on athletic fields, a climb to rock-strewn summits, encampments pitched by bubbling springs, steaming chocolate, sizzling bacon, the glow of the evening campfire, stories told of trial and adventure, a night in the open—such experiences and a multitude of others fall to the lot of Winona campers.

*An early brochure, circa 1910.*

(decorative tree border)

### CHARACTER BUILDING

Though we make sure of giving our boys a bully good time, and of having them grow straight and strong, alert, and vigorous, yet the chief insistence at Greylock is to train the boys in those virtues that every mother and father wish to see their son possess.

(decorative tree border)

*From a 1920 Greylock brochure.*

*One classic camp recruiting device has been to stress cultural values. One of the Wigwam founders, Abraham Mandelstam, was given to having his picture taken with various luminaries and distributing the photos to parents of campers and prospective campers. A parent might infer from this that if his son went to Wigwam he too might associate with people like Einstein.*

APPLICATION FORM.

## SUMMER VACATION, 1886.

I desire to attend the Y. M. C. A. BOYS' CAMP. I will undertake the requisite course of study, pass the required examination, and agree to whatever conditions and rules may be deemed best. I enclose fifteen cents, for which send me the set of pamphlets to be studied.

Paid

Geo.f.Weller

Newburgh N.Y.

Secretaries please approve and forward to S. F. DUDLEY, Box 2849, N. Y.

Y. M. C. A. BOYS' CAMP.

*An eager lad applied with this card for the second season at the YMCA camp, later renamed Camp Dudley. One question on the entrance exam was "How many of the Bible stories have you read?" Among rules to be obeyed included, "Boys will not be permitted to bring dogs to camp."*

The Camp is meant only for gentlemanly, well-bred boys who will be interested to carry out its purpose. They must not mind a little roughness and must be ready to contribute their share toward the good fellowship and success of the Camp.

Once all the directors had come and gone, all you were left with was a pile of brochures. These were glorifications of camp facilities and manifestos of camp philosophy designed to make the camp sound at least different, if not better, than the others.

According to the brochures, almost all camps were "secluded yet accessible" with "extensive camp property" (an acreage count was generally provided) and "sandy soil and subsoil to insure perfect drainage." "Spring-fed lakes" were "sheltered from severe storms by low, encircling hills," and were, you were assured, "checked regularly by the Board of Health."

The sleeping quarters were variously described. Often they represented "the last word in modern camp equipment," with "fine, comfortable structures completely screened." (When you arrived at camp you discovered that they neglected to tell you the screens were in lieu of glass in the windows, and only shutters kept out the rain—but unfortunately when closed, also shut out the light.) A brochure for a more rugged, woodsier camp leveled with the prospective camper, declaring, "The shanties are rough but give sufficient shelter." Cabins were *always* described as well-ventilated, a fact that would be denied by no camper who ever had to get out of bed on a cold, damp morning.

Camp climate was "invigorating and healthful." It was also "especially palliative to sufferers from hay fever." The air was "pure, dry, and bracing." Ragweed was virtually unknown.

The main function of the brochures, with all their hyperbole, was to help you keep the "facts" straight when you sat down to make your decision. The process of how that final decision was actually reached usually remained slightly mysterious. But the fact of the matter was, by the end of the winter, it *had* been decided. You were going to camp!

4

*Naturally everyone is interested in the look of the camp. Photographs of tent or cabin rows nestled up to the trees help to conjure up an idyllic setting.*

*Music is an important element of the cultural program, as this typical photo of a girls' chorus running through a number illustrates.*

**Camp** **Wigwam**
*A Summer Camp for Boys*

HARRISON
MAINE

FOUNDED NINETEEN TEN

ARNOLD M. LEHMAN
666 WEST END AVENUE, NEW YORK 25, N.Y.
TELEPHONE SChuyler 4-0346
ABRAHAM MANDELSTAM
40 WEST 72ND STREET, NEW YORK 23, N.Y.
TELEPHONE ENdicott 2-6100

New York 25, New York
February 17, 1958

Hello, Richard,

Surely you must know that your mother and dad have just
enrolled you to be one of our Wigwam boys next summer, so I
gladly welcome you into our camp family.  I want you to know
that you **can count** on me to be your pal and a real "Pop" to
you throughout **every** day of your entire season at Wigwam.
Please be sure to come to me for anything at all that I can
do to make this the top-notch summer of your whole life; for
you know that, as one of the directors of the camp, it's my
job to see that everybody is happy.

During every minute of the time that you will be enjoying with us, you should be thinking:  "I have the very best
mother and dad in all the world for giving me such a wonderful summer."  You can now look forward to a rousing good
time with a fine bunch of fellows from North, East, South,
and West, under the leadership of real boys' men and in a
boys' world, built to order especially for them.  How's that
for a dandy combination?  You will find that the more of yourself you put into Wigwam, the more will Wigwam be able to do
for you in return.

Every Wigwamer likes to have his camp pennant hanging
in his room; so I am **now** mailing one for you to enjoy with
our compliments.

Here's to many happy camping days together this summer;
and if, in the meantime, an opportunity should arise for us
to see each other, I shall be much pleased indeed.

Mrs. Lehman and I send warm regards to you and your folks.

Ever yours,

*Pop Lehman*

Arnold M. Lehman

AML/jht

*A depths-of-winter letter to a soon-to-be new camper letting him know he'll be one of the crowd.*

Your packs and hatchets, bats and rackets, now lie idle. Look them over! Inspect your camp kits! For days are fleeting and soon again Winona will assemble friends of old and campers new to hike and swim, and ride and row, to fish, explore and build encampments.

In the winter of 1922, this effusive missive was received by all Winona campers of the previous season. Such reminders of the past and future joys of camp were an attempt to keep the upcoming season always in mind. Special birthday cards, Christmas cards, and Easter cards flooded the mail and implied that, even if, for some reason, you weren't thinking about camp, camp was thinking about you.

For those children who helped pay their own way, camp was unquestionably on their minds all year 'round. Some sang in the church choir, and in return the church would pay for a week at Camp Andover or Waldron. If you went to either of the YMCA camps, Ousamequin or Dorchester, in 1934, you were encouraged to sell old papers and bottles to a junk dealer to raise money. With this money you could purchase camp stamps at a nickel apiece to paste into your camp stamp book (a system similar to blue chip stamps). When the book was filled—and you could also get camp stamps for birthdays or Christmas—you would have $12 to apply toward your camp fee of $17.50 for two weeks.

In 1935, campers at Ousamequin received the following letter encouraging thrift:

Camp time can't come too soon for most of us! It seems a long way off right now, with the thermometer "percolating" dangerously near the zero mark. BUT have you started to save for your stay at camp? We don't want you to be one of the fellows who says at the first spell of hot weather, when everyone is talking about going off to camp, "I wish I'd saved my pennies so I could go to camp, too."

Start today to drop those nickels and dimes in your bank. Did you know that if you put a dime away every day from now until the first of July you'd have enough to take care of two weeks at camp? Isn't that worth striving for?

As spring approached, campers and camp directors conducted a flurry of communications pertinent to the upcoming season. Old-time campers knew definitely whom they wanted or didn't as bunkmates, and all this information had to be relayed to the director. Some veterans even tried—with some

*Camp would have been remiss if off-season birthday wishes had not been sent.*

*Twenty cents' worth of YMCA stamps ready to be pasted into the camp stamp book to help earn your way.*

## NORTH WOODS CAMP

### A Summer Camp *for* Boys

#### On Lake Winnepesaukee

**JANUARY 1934**

| S | M | T | W | T | F | S |
|---|---|---|---|---|---|---|
| ... | 1 | 2 | 3 | 4 | 5 | 6 |
| 7 | 8 | 9 | 10 | 11 | 12 | 13 |
| 14 | 15 | 16 | 17 | 18 | 19 | 20 |
| 21 | 22 | 23 | 24 | 25 | 26 | 27 |
| 28 | 29 | 30 | 31 | ... | ... | ... |

Directors

Gilbert H. Roehrig    Francis L. Moginot

316 Huntington Avenue    Boston, Massachusetts

*A Christmastime reminder for campers of the good old days of summer at North Woods.*

success—to assure that they'd get a certain counselor. From the camp came the reminders to take your physical exam and to get all your shots. There were packing lists; there was travel information; there were special notices, perhaps of a change in canteen policy, or a stern reminder that absolutely "NO PENKNIVES may be brought to camp."

Forms also came home to be filled out by campers and their parents on what activities were priorities that summer. For some this meant the yearly battle of what you wanted to do versus what your parents thought you should be "exposed" to: "All right, you can take fencing *only* if you agree to take sailing." Parents would admonish their children not to avoid the waterfront: "Your mother and I would really appreciate it if you could pass your thirty-minute deep-water test this summer." Many camps offered "extras," such as horseback riding and long mountain-climbing trips, which involved an additional charge. Other extras may not have cost more but still required parental permission: aquaplaning—perceived as dangerous by some parents but as an absolute necessity by their kids.

Amid these final arrangements, your camp clothes arrived from the outfitter. If you'd ordered early enough, the camp outfitters sewed all your name tapes in for you. Otherwise your mother was sewing them in up to the last minute. (By the early 1960s modern technology had provided "boilproof cement" for those articles not amenable to sewing.) The rules were strict. Everything you took to camp—and anything sent to you later—had to be marked on the inside top of each garment. The name tape had to be sewn *all* the way around on *all* four edges, not just at the two ends, a shortcut favored by some mothers. Furthermore, they could not be placed over another label. Each shoe and rubber was to be marked on the inside with indelible ink.

If the camp didn't have a uniform, just what the outfit should (or shouldn't) be was always spelled out. A good example from 1902 is the letter sent to campers going to Camp Agassiz in the High Sierras: "The camp is a place to wear out old clothes, the traveling suit is good enough for the dressiest occasion. The essentials are flannel shirts, canvas overalls, hunting coat, sweater, hobnailed shoes, and leggins." Similarly, at Marienfeld Camp during that same era, the outfit was simple, with boys wearing ". . . the least clothing the weather permits, no hats, and preferably no shoes and stockings."

*(Tune: "Why Shouldn't We?")*

*The thing they call vacation's in the air,*
*This is the time of year when everywhere*
*Kids start to rummage for bloomers and sneaks,*
*Stretch out their muscles and oil up their squeaks.*
—Camp Walden

## LORDY WHAT A HUMMER
*(Tune: "Carolina in the Morning")*

*Lordy, what a hummer of a time I*
*    have each summer,*
*Up at Greylock: How could life be*
*    sweeter or more joyous or completer*
*Than at Greylock*
*When the sun is shining*
*Where the hemlocks sway,*
*My poor heart is pining*
*All through the livelong day.*
*Just to see the batter tap his*
*    bat upon the platter*
*Up at Greylock*
*How the voices singing 'round the*
*    campfire come arringing*
*From old Greylock.*
*If I had Alladin's lamp I'd rub*
*    it and cry . . .*
*"Genie, make my life eternal July."*
*Lordy, what a hummer of a time I*
*    have each summer*
*Up at Greylock.*

## WE ARE BANDED LIKE BIRDS

*We are banded like birds to return*
*    in July,*
*We are happy as larks back to Wigwam*
*    to fly.*
*We are friends reunited from most*
*    anywhere;*
*What a joy to be free and to breathe*
*    Wigwam air.*

## I'M OFF TO CAMP SOMERSET
*(Tune: "Oh, Susannah")*

*I packed my trunk the other night,*
*I mailed my duffle bag.*
*I sewed name-tapes on all my clothes,*
*Yes, even my washrag.*

*Chorus:*
*Brothers, sisters now don't you cry for me,*
*I'm off to Camp Somerset,*
*As happy as can be.*

## TALL GIRLS SHORT GIRLS

*Tall girls, short girls*
*Fat and thin.*
*Whatcha gonna do when the heat comes in*
*Nothin to do, nothin to say*
*Now's the time to pack your bags*
*And go away.*
*Come to Tapawingo where the breezes blow*
*Come to Tapawingo where you swim and row*
*Answer the ever loving call*
*Come to Tapawingo, the best of all.*

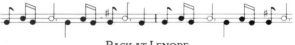

## BACK AT LENORE

*Summer brings joy to each camper's heart,*
*Taking us back to Lenore.*
*Long happy days after months apart,*
*Playing together once more.*
*The sun that warms us, the birds that sing,*
*The hills and the winding shore,*
*All taken together mean just one thing—*
*Here we are back at Lenore!*

*When summer is over and we go home,*
*Backward our thoughts will stray*
*To the green hills we loved to roam,*
*Happy at work or at play.*
*The lake of silver, the skies so blue,*
*Will stay with us evermore.*
*Although we can't have them the whole year through,*
*They'll carry us back to Lenore!*

*A collection of songs written to foment the camp spirit during the off-season. These were sung at reunions, before camp started,*
*and even on the trip to camp. They were to be found in almost any camp songster.*

Uniform camps were much stricter than their counterparts. The standard outfit for boys was shorts—usually gray, with a camp color ribboned down the sides—and T-shirts with the camp insignia or name emblazoned across the front. Girls' camps could get quite fancy, requiring not only the uniform shorts and shirts, but also blazers, vests, ties, and the occasional beret to top it off for dress occasions. By 1940, to the delight of most young girls, middies, bloomers, and long stockings had been universally shed. The rule of thumb was "to expose as much of the body to the sun as is modestly possible."

There have always been camps that have favored uniforms and those that have eschewed them. An early argument on behalf of uniforms came from the Sebago-Wohelo Camps during the teens:

Uniformity of costume does for the camp just what the uniform does for the army, namely: promotes the feeling of team spirit, puts all on the same level, and avoids color conflicts which are irritating to sensitive people. A group of charming girls in beautiful uniform is a thrilling sight, thrilling not only to the spectator but to the girls themselves.

*The hiking outfit and "knockabout" uniform offered by the A. G. Spalding Company in 1921.*

Finally, all that remained was packing. First on the agenda was digging out your camp blankets from their mothballed storage place. These could air out for a day or two before being stuffed in a duffel bag with linens, pillow, boots, and shoes. Almost every camper used a footlocker for his or her clothing. These came with a compartmentalized tray inside, the pros and cons of which were debatable. Although ideal for storage of small items, such as a flashlight and extra batteries, a can of 6-12 insect repellent, and a deck of cards—all of which would otherwise undoubtedly gravitate to the bottom of the trunk—the tray took up trunk space, which was at a premium, and *always* had to be removed whenever you wanted to get anything out.

A boy scout camper from the thirties recalled packing his gear for his first summer away from home. His uncle, an old navy man, convinced him of the superiority of a duffel bag over a trunk. After two weeks of rummaging through his bag, and having to dump it out every time he wanted something, he swore off duffel bags. He never took one to camp again.

Your mom always packed your trunk according to the packing list. Three copies of the list were filled out with all your belongings indicated: One was pasted on the inside lid of the trunk, one filed in the camp office, and the other stayed home.

Besides the everyday wear for play and dress, there was a multitude of items that could be construed as necessities: "two natural rubber bathing caps," "one olive poncho, size 66 inches by 90 inches," two laundry bags, one dozen handkerchiefs or a supply of tissues, and preaddressed and stamped postcards for your parents and grandparents. By this point the trunk was close to overflowing, but you had to find nooks and crannies in which to squish the extras: the canoe pillow, a masquerade costume, your game of Clue, your Brownie camera and film, and the "frogman" equipment.

Because food packages from home were taboo at many camps, it was only natural to stash a few articles of contraband edibles in the trunk as well. A Tripp Lake camper from the 1950s recalled the regulation at her camp that once you reached a certain age you were allowed to bring from home all the food you wanted to. You were not allowed to replenish your supply during the season and any food your parents sent or brought to camp would be confiscated (with the exception of fresh fruit on Visitor's Day). The trick was to try to bring enough food to last eight weeks and still leave room for your clothing. So girls stocked up on the basic fare of tuna, sardines, and crackers. Those with educated tastes even brought anchovies. Candy and gum, however, were not allowed. Recently campers have been stretching the rule to its limits. In 1981, one girl sent two duffel bags to camp, one filled only with food, including forty cans of tuna. The director commented that at the beginning of the season, the girl's tent interior looked like a 7-Eleven market.

With two weeks to go before camp started, labels were filled out with the camp address and pasted onto trunks or tied onto duffel bags. Then the baggage was carted off to Railway Express for its long journey to camp. Any forgotten items had to be hand carried to camp on departure day.

*And all this fit into your trunk and duffel bag?*

---

## Season 1932

CL

# Tripp Lake Camp
### Poland, Maine

## REQUIREMENTS FOR CAMPERS

Each camper must be provided with one complete T. L. C. Off Campus and On Campus uniform. Articles starred *must* be bought from the Official Outfitter. Other articles listed may be bought from the Outfitter if desired. OLD CAMPERS ARE REQUESTED NOT TO PURCHASE ANY PART OF THE NEW OUTFIT UNLESS THE NEW ARTICLES ARE NEEDED.

### Off Campus Uniform
*1 pr. T. L. C. Bloomers
*1 T. L. C. Middie
*1 T. L. C. Kerchief
*1 T. L. C. Beret
*1 T. L. C. Sweater (slip-on style)

*3 prs. T. L. C. Hose
*1 Regulation Green Wool Jersey
1 pr. T. L. C. Oxford Moccasins (Fitted at Camp)

### On Campus Uniform
*3 prs. Regulation Blue Bloomers (flannel)—new style
*8 Regulation Fitted White Middie Shirts—new style
*1 Regulation Tan Leather T.L.C. Belt—new
2 prs. High White Sneakers

1 pr. High Rubbers to fit Sneakers (fitted at Camp)
*10 prs. Anklet Sox
2 Regulation T. L. C. Bathing Suits, with strap across back—new style
1 pr. Rubber Bathing Slippers
1 Regulation Blue Wool Jersey (optional)

The following articles will complete the outfit:

6 Suits Athletic Underwear
1 pr. Dancing Sandals
4 prs. Pajamas (thin and heavy)
1 Heavy Bathrobe
1 pr. Bedroom Slippers
2 prs. Round Garters
Bathing Caps (should be purchased at Camp)
1 Raincoat or Slicker
1 Plain Cotton Smock
1 Coat Hanger and Dress Bag
1 Mess Kit
1 Medium Weight Knapsack
1 pr. Riding Breeches

1 Pack Strap for Hiking Trips
1 Poncho
1 Duffel Bag with Lock
6 Single Sheets
4 Pillow Cases
1 Pillow
4 Wash Cloths
6 Face Towels
6 Bath Towels
2 Laundry Bags with Name
1 T. L. C. Wool Blanket with Monogram
2 Single Heavy Wool Blankets Name Tapes

EVERY ARTICLE, INCLUDING THOSE WORN TO CAMP, MUST BE PLAINLY MARKED WITH NAME TAPES.

*The yearly scene at Grand Central Station, New York City (top), complete with signs, excited campers, and apprehensive parents. In 1953, 36,000 campers left from this station in two days' time. Transportation details were always a headache—two pre-camp communiques passed the vital information on to the campers.*

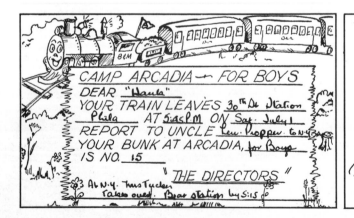

CAMP ARCADIA → FOR BOYS
DEAR "*Hank*"
YOUR TRAIN LEAVES 30ᵗʰ St. Station
Phila AT 5:45 P.M ON Sat. July 1
REPORT TO UNCLE Lew. Propper to N.Y.
YOUR BUNK AT ARCADIA, for Boys
IS NO. 15
"THE DIRECTORS"
At N.Y. Mrs. Tucker
Takes over. Bear station by 5:15

### TRIPP LAKE CAMP SPECIAL
LEAVES PENNSYLVANIA STATION
NEW YORK CITY

NORTH END OF MAIN CONCOURSE, UPPER LEVEL
AT ENTRANCE TO TUNNEL TO HOTEL NEW YORKER.

THURSDAY, JUNE 30, 1932
5:30 P. M. EASTERN STANDARD TIME
6:30 P. M. DAYLIGHT SAVING TIME

*Maxine Hirsch*
NAME OF CAMPER
12-6

CAR No. *9*
BERTH No. *10*

# Getting There

Traditionally, the camp season began the day before the first day. Getting there, if not half the fun, was surely an event in itself. From the early 1900s to the late 1960s, the camp train was *the* bona fide method of transport. It has now largely given way to the airplane and the bus.

The last-minute freneticism of piling into the car in your new camp clothes, with overnight bag, tennis racquet, baseball mitt, and five dollars spending money, was the beginning of the long, often sleepless, journey to camp. En route to the station came the battery of questions: "What's the name of your counselor? Where is your trunk key? Do you have your allergy medicine? Will you *please* remember to write?"

The scene at the station was always a madhouse—a million and one kids and two million and two parents milling around under the respective camp banners. You scanned the horizon for the name of your camp, and when it was spotted, ran to meet old friends—unless, of course, it was your first year, in which case you approached the unknown more timidly.

Then the "All aboard!" call was given, and it was time for tearful good-byes, promises to write, and last-minute admonitions. "Watch out for the poison ivy!" It was at this point that many new campers got their first twinges of homesickness. In 1935, the *New York Times* reported, "Little boys who refused to part with their dogs caused bedlam." Even for first-timers, however, the excitement of an overnight train ride was usually enough to quell misgivings about leaving home. Recalled one camper:

I was seven when I was first bundled off to North Carolina. I wasn't particularly keen on the idea of spending two months away from home but the idea of an overnight train ride intrigued me. I mean, for years my only ambition in life was to be a train engineer, and I considered the trip down and back to be what my summer was all about. The eight weeks in the middle was merely a rest stop while they turned the train around. So what happens, I get stuck in the upper bunk with no windows. Right away I wanted to go back.

But there was no going back. A few campers have been known to leave at midseason, but practically no one has left before arriving.

When the first excitement died down and the scramble for seats was over, everyone settled in with comic books and movie magazines. In the 1930s, Camp Androscoggin plied its campers

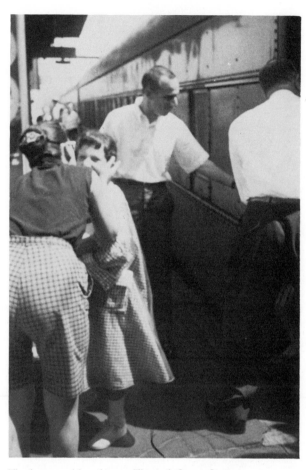

*The last good-bye kiss at Thirtieth Street Station, Philadelphia.*

*The lower berth on the Bar Harbor Express headed for Camp Fernwood.*

*Stealing train signs was a favorite diversion en route. The most coveted: "Do not flush while train is in station."*

with *Lone Ranger* magazines to ward off potential mischief. But no diversion was enough to stop the visiting back and forth, the card games, prank playing, and running amok that were the order of the day—and the night. Certainly there was little anyone could do to stave off the annual water pistol battle at bedtime. Campers are nothing if not traditional.

In 1952, a ten-year-old veteran camper penned a quick note home at one-thirty in the morning:

I am having a great time on the train, as usual I am staying up all night. I won fifteen cents playing poker and still going. I met alot of boys I like . . . Howare my fish? . . . Be sure and send me my flash atichement and bulbs and batteries. Okay for now.

It was often obligatory to write your parents from the train. Anyway, this was a good time to request forgotten items after everyone else on the train told you what they'd brought along. On the other hand, who really wanted to take the time out from having fun to write? A girl at Alford Lake Camp described the chore in the camp log of 1940:

Then the usual custom of writing to either or both our parents. Postcards and pencils were passed out. All started thinking hard of what to say. Room was very skillfully utilized, though, by saying, "Excuse my writing, but the train is very bumpy." With a few more words this short, but of course sweet, epistle was ended.

One thing to look forward to was mealtime. Depending on what camp you went to, in what era, and where you got on the train, dinner could be anything from roast beef in the diner to a box lunch consisting of sandwiches, fruit, leaky cartons of chocolate milk, and Hershey chocolate bars. A wartime camper wrote in 1945: "The tuna fish sandwiches were very delicious aside from the fact that there was no tuna fish in them."

A lucky few got to eat in the dining car, and because they had to walk through many cars en route, they could visit around and perhaps even swap comic books with kids from other camps.

As a rule, though, you were confined to your camp cars—a rule that no doubt intensified the prank playing that began in earnest after dinner.

Dear Mom & Dad, I am in the train and having lots of fun. Mike is in my berth with me. We're going to raid berth's to-

14

*It may be a long and bumpy journey from the train station to the camp, but it's worth it.*

Morning—Glimpses of green woods and cool waters. Somerset draws nearer, nearer, nearer. Oh, the last half-hour! Minutes seem more like hours; seconds drag by till the first roof-tops of Oakland straggle into view.

And the arrival—Eddie and Sam are greeting us. Trucks and taxies wait to carry impatient campers to their destination. Somerset at last. The season is started.

*From the Camp Somerset publication,* Somer = Settings, *volume 2, number 1, 1929.*

### IT'S A LONG WAY TO CAMP ABNAKI
*(Tune: "It's a Long Way to Tipperary")*

*Up to Camp Abnaki*
*We are coming year by year,*
*Representing country towns*
*And cities far and near;*
*Fat boys, lean boys, tall boys, short boys,*
*Every kind, you see,*
*In many things we differ,*
*But in this we all agree—*

*Chorus:*
*It's a long way to Camp Abnaki*
*It's a long way to go;*
*It's a long way to Camp Abnaki,*
*To the best boys' camp I know,*
*Good-bye little dairy,*
*Farewell, city's glare,*
*It's a long, long way to Camp Abnaki,*
*But my heart's right there.*

Camp Abnaki Handbook, *1921.*

*The Bell Telephone Company preprinted information post-cards for camps to send home upon the campers' arrival. This "service" also promoted toll calls from parents.*

night. . . . We are in Hartford, Conn. right now. It is about 11:30 P.M. We were having alot of fun. I'm reading comic's and fooling around, they blame me for everything that happen's and I don't like it. Soon we'll get to Portland and we'll almost be there.

Another mischief maker, headed for Camp Horseshoe in Wisconsin in the late 1950s, recalled tying pull-firecrackers to the curtains of each berth in the car.

Campers were usually bedded two to a berth, as a girl from Alford Lake wrote:

For some of the Alford Lake Campers, Saturday dawned in a spacious lower berth with a nice window to gaze out, but for other less privileged ones it began in an upper berth with no outlook save a sooty ventilator, and the problem of sliding or leaping down to the floor of the car.

Breakfast came in cardboard boxes. There were, no doubt, many to whom it was a simple affair, but there were some expert orange-juice squirters in one car.

If you arrived at your station before breakfast you had the additional treat of eating at a local hotel before continuing on to camp. The Hotel Eastland, in Portland, was one such watering hole for campers in southern Maine.

For those campers headed farther north, toward the Belgrade or Rangely Lake districts, Portland meant a layover—time for nearby camps to disembark their campers. During this time the trainmen switched cars around and put together trains that

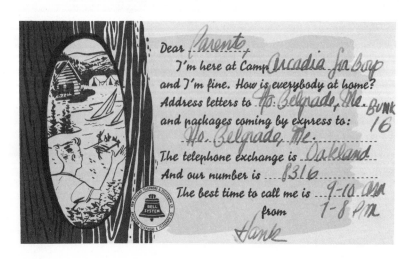

would go to the different areas. This was usually around dawn. Occasionally campers were known to sneak out of their Pullmans in pajamas and bare feet to procure some goodies to eat from Armstrong's, the all-night restaurant in Union Station. Unfortunately, because of the switchings, when they returned, their cars were not always where they had left them. Every year a number of badly frightened campers would be rounded up by railroad passenger representatives. These men, accustomed to this yearly occurrence, simply checked name tapes, complete with camp names, sewn into everyone's pj's and delivered them to the right trains.

Eventually you reached your destination—the station closest to camp. Here would be "a curious collection of school buses of uncertain vintage, several open-bodied trucks and even a two-horse hay wagon to assist in getting the kids to camp: a case of using what was available," recalled a Boston & Maine railroadman.

After the kids disembarked, train crews and porters searched through each car to gather all the lost belongings—cameras, comic books, jackets, and baseball caps. This booty was turned over to the respective camps, with the slight prospect that some of it would be reclaimed.

Obviously not every camper had the joy of the overnight. Those who lived too close to camp got only a simple train ride with either a box lunch or a meal at the hotel. And some unfortunates never got to ride the train at all. Those within striking distance (or not near the train route) were often driven directly to camp by their parents. A South Carolinian recalled his North Carolina camp days in the 1950s:

Camp Catawba was a curious place. Its residents came by way of Hickory on a train whose interior I could only imagine. Although I, contrariwise, traveled north and by car, the train to me was as much a part of Catawba as the morning assembly. Yet this train remained for me an object of fantasy. The interior of the garage, the counselors' room, even the back rooms in the Mainhouse were mysteries that sooner or later I came to observe first-hand. The train stayed forever remote in my imagination.

During the last leg of the journey, as the motley camp vehicles ground their gears on hilly country roads leading from the train station to the camp, the singing of camp songs helped pass the time. Old-time campers kept a sharp lookout for landmarks. One was the Howard Johnson's at the base of Long Lake in Naples, Maine, a much-valued stopping place, where, over the years, countless ice-cream cones were consumed.

Shouts went up at the first sighting of a signpost for camp. From there the contest was on: Who could first spot the beach from across the lake, the roof of the lodge, or the totem pole? As the entrance came into view the familiar chant began: "Free,

*You're really at camp when you pass through the main gate.*

*More than just your overnight bag had to be toted to camp: your baseball mitt, tennis racquet, golf clubs, and lanyard were just as important. Arrival at Camp Dudley in the early 1960s.*

17

Free, Free, Free . . ." and then, as the gates were passed, "Slaves!"

Exploding from the buses the campers ran around the grounds renewing old ties with their summer home—down to the lake—up to the lodge—off to the special spots in camp: the Old Pine at Wicosuta; the Maysie Tree at Wigwam; Point Point at Kehonka; Twin Pines at Walden. . . .

Those first few minutes were hardest for new campers. They didn't know where to run. A Waldenite described the feeling in the 1980 *Splash*:

> The soft rumble of buses slowly comes into being,
> With me upon one, what am I seeing?
> Happy young girls reminiscing about summers past,
> Thinking of how it all went so fast.
> Talking of how this year would be better,
> They take no notice of my Camp Walden sweater,
> And walk right past me to greet others that are known,
> I really and truely felt all alone.
> Until an old camper says, "Are you new?"
> "Yes," I say, "I'm in bunk 2."
> Suddenly I feel very close and near,
> To this friendly place called Walden.

Settling in wasn't always easy. It involved wandering around, forming first impressions, asking endless questions of the counselors, meeting new kids. One eight-year-old camper's first letter home during a season in the 1940s revealed strong opinions: "One conciler seems to be a smart Alec, I don't like him. He will probably be public Camp Arcadia counciler Enemy No. 1. He is Uncle Joe. I like Uncle Norman though." The following year, his first impressions were just as strong:

> Dear Mom + Dad, I arrived this morning, and got assigned to bunk 16. The boy's in my bunk are: Frank "Dopey", Richard "The Nut", Dickey "The Duck", Gerry "Woo-Woo" and I. My councilor's are: Uncle Ronny and Uncle Bob. I don't like Uncle Ronny or Frank "The Dope" & I mean The Dope. I am all unpacked and all accounted for. My activety today is Baseball. . . . Please send up my Report Card. I had an argument and I want to prove I am right about getting an A+ +. I'll send it back then.

By the next day, the program was set, the activities started, and the campers "at home" or fighting off homesickness. The season was underway.

*A few of the camps near Harrison, Maine.*

### In the Old Days

In the early days of camping, you could never be sure what, if anything, would be down at the station to take you on the last lap of your trip. Camp "conveyances" often were so dilapidated that campers refused to ride in them, preferring to walk—or run—instead. Boys headed for Camp Yawgoog in Rhode Island in 1916 were carried for several hours in an open truck with backless benches. On steep hills, however, they'd get out and walk, as it was faster than riding up in the truck.

The tradition at Camp Kennebec in Maine was to hike three miles from the train station to the camp over rutted dirt roads. Up until the late 1930s this was done in city clothes, which would then be stored at camp in mothballs for the return trip. In 1938 the tradition was changed and campers entrained already wearing their camp uniforms, leaving city clothes home where they belonged.

Some camps were so remote that there were no roads to them. At the Winona Camps in Maine this was true until at least 1930. A reminder was sent to parents: "People traveling to camp by automobile should come to Denmark Village for motor boat connections as there are no roads direct to the Winona Camps." The directions to the Luther Gulick Camps were even more elaborate. First a steamer was taken from New York to Boston, then a train to Portland, a switch to another train for the Sebago Lake Station, and finally, from there a steamer would circle the lake, dropping the girls off on the rocks at the shore of the camps.

Perhaps the strangest sight, though, was the arrival of the boys at Camp Waldron in New Hampshire for the first season in 1926. The roads to the camp were not yet passable, so camp war canoes loaded high with boys and duffel bags were towed behind the motor launch.

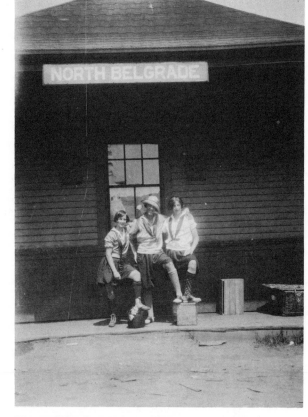

*Waiting for pickup to Camp Runoia, circa 1925.*

*Arrival at the Luther Gulick Camps in 1917.*

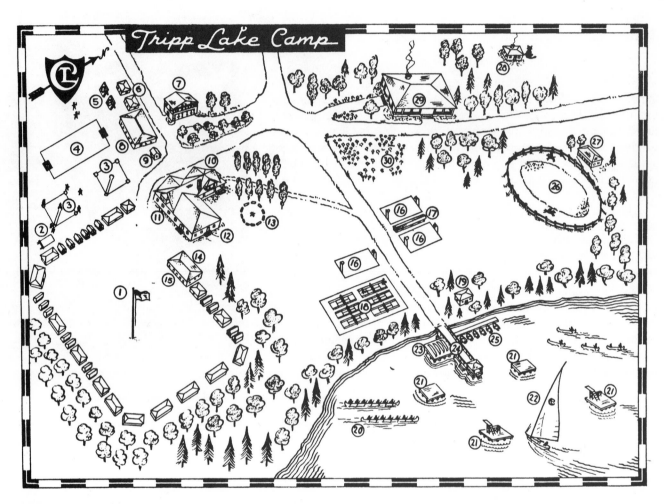

*Tripp Lake Camp*

**KEY TO MAP**

1. Campus (surrounded by tents and bungalows)
2. Tennis practice board
3. Baseball diamonds
4. Hockey field
5. Archery range
6. Tool houses
7. Garage and service quarters
8. Laundry and service quarters
9. Ice house
10. Administration, office, infirmary
11. Kitchen
12. Dining porch
13. Campfire circle
14. Arts and crafts studio
15. Wash house—hot shower room
16. Basketball courts
17. Pavilion
18. Tennis courts
19. Paddle house
20. "War" canoes
21. Diving floats and rafts
22. Sailboat
23. Canoe float
24. Swimming pier
25. Rowboat dock
26. Riding paddock
27. Stable
28. "Kitty's" House
29. Recreation building ("Over the Wall")
30. Flower garden

*Large or small, in a woodland setting or spread over the hills and fields, most camps foster feelings of hominess and security. Many provide bird's eye views in their brochures. The scale is often puzzling, with tents the same size as tennis courts and war canoes longer than basketball courts, but the feel of the camp is there.*

# Behold the Camp

The camp always seemed immense—larger, certainly, than it turned out to be if you revisited it in later years. Of course, some camps are gigantic—a thousand acres or more—but size is all relative. When you were a child, and it was dark, and you had to go back from the lodge to your tent all by yourself to get the sweater you'd forgotten, it seemed like *forever*.

During the summer, camp was your whole world, and you gradually established a special intimacy with its geography. You came to think in time that during all those summers there nothing could have escaped your notice. But the fact is, some areas always did remain a mystery. The upstairs rooms in the lodge —you never did look in them all. And that strange locked shed down behind the baseball diamond—what was that about? Odd, that you never got around to checking everything out. Too busy.

It didn't matter if your camp had tents, cabins, or big bunk-houses, or if they were strung out in a neat row or sprinkled through the woods; camp had a look and feel that was all its own. The blending of the site and architecture, along with many seasons of campers and counselors, who left behind their indelible imprints, resulted in the special environment that was camp.

The layout depended most heavily on the lay of the land. Open spaces dictated where the playing fields went. If there was a hill, and there usually was, the dining hall always seemed to be at the top of it, no small nuisance for the camp population three times each day.

Some camp founders had strong feelings about the way a camp should look. Gilbert H. Roehrig, who established Camp North Woods, believed no buildings should be visible from out on the lake, and heavy woods screened all structures from sight. Ironically, after Roehrig's death, a building in his memory was placed right on the waterfront. Some camps took advantage of the great view at the water's edge, stringing their cabins and tents along the shores—trading scenic vistas for a slightly colder sleeping experience.

Most camps had a general consistency of architectural style, and the smallest storage building tended to be remarkably reminiscent of a sleeping cabin, which in turn closely resembled the nature lodge. This uniformity of vision surpassed the actual materials of which the buildings were constructed.

Rustic design was almost always employed to some degree.

*Nestled among the pines, or right at the water's edge, the cabins and tents at Camp Kehonka give campers great views, plenty of privacy, and a feeling of living in the out-of-doors.*

Camp signs are often ambitious works of art, which can tell more about the place than at first meets the eye. The rustic "Camp Kehonka," made of natural saplings, is an indication at the gate of the rustic architecture within. The brightly painted "Camp Watitoh," carved in the woodshop, reflects the camp's coed population.

Waldenites, proud of their camp name, had their camp photo taken in the traditional W formation.

## SPELLING IT OUT

The derivation of camp names could itself constitute an entire branch of science.

Indian names abound. Some are chosen for their meaning: Una-layee, Cherokee for "place of friends"; Tapawingo, an Indian word for "place of joy"; Chautauqua, Seneca for "one who has taken out fish here."

Sometimes the name has a nice ring to it, but the meaning is a bit off: Chippewa, "to roast until puckered up," is a good recipe for marshmallows, but not an apt description, one hopes, for a camp.

In some instances the true meaning of the Indian word must not have been looked into when the name was chosen. Winona, a Sioux word for "female first born," seems like an odd choice for a boys' camp. Camp Winnebago, located on beautiful Echo Lake, is named for the Chippewa word meaning "dirty water." And Camp Adirondack, where the food is probably no worse than any other camp, is named for the Sioux word meaning "they eat trees."

Hyphenated names might add an Indian flavor: Taik-Ur-Eez; As-You-Like-It; Sun-O-Set; and Ha-Wa-Ya. Sometimes even the hyphen is dispensed with, as in Kairphree.

When, perhaps, imagination has failed, camps have been named after the owner or his children: The Cheley Colorado Camps; Dr. Johnson's Camps; Kennolyn, a shortened version of Kenneth and Carolyn; and Trebor, Robert spelled backward.

STICK FIGURES

*Rustic buildings and furnishings are natural for camps. The woods are searched for saplings with the right curves and bends, and for straight pieces of the proper thickness and length. Benches, tables, and fences are frequently constructed in rustic fashion. The library at Camp Kehonka (upper left) is filled with rustic items, including light fixtures and built-in furniture. The lodge at Camp Wigwam (upper right) makes use of a colonnade of tree trunks and a porch filled with rustic chairs. The Bucklin Memorial Lodge at Camp Yawgoog (lower left) has a stairway built of split logs resting on whole logs, with sapling bannisters. Camp Winnebago is sprinkled with handsome examples of rustic furniture, such as this bench (lower right).*

*Rustic cabins, even shingled ones, can give a camp a good, rugged feeling, but tents add a primitive flavor that cannot be beat. Although the director may point out that cabins provide better shelter, look neater, and last longer, tent dwellers prefer their airy shelters, even if it means hiking to the bathroom and a greater risk of rain-damaged belongings.*

Log cabins were one of the most familiar conventions. Slabsided buildings, covered with thin lengths cut from trees with the bark left on, provided a very woodsy look. And then there was the rustic furniture. Chairs, benches, and tables were made of saplings, branches, and the occasional tree stump. "Authentic" rustic furniture was always made by hand, with no machined wood. All joints were carved or notched together. In the rough-and-tumble camp environment, however, slats would come loose from the chair backs or seats and eventually get lost before they were replaced, adding greatly to the discomfort of anyone who dared sit in them. (Rustic furniture could be comfortable, despite its looks.)

Rustication notwithstanding, some camps also affected distinctive regional styles. Camp Waldemar in Texas showed the combined influence of the southwestern Indian, Mexican design, and a cowboy spirit in its buildings of quarry tile, stone, and decorative ceramic tile. Camp Kennolyn in California, on the site of a former logging mill, reflected an Old West town theme in its layout and building design.

The character of a camp was often embodied in its lodge, generally a cavernous multipurpose structure built of local materials. At one time there were master craftsmen who specialized in building these massive lodges, using trees from the campgrounds for the exposed post and beam construction, notching them together for the sides, splitting them into shingles for the roof, and using the branches for balustrades and balconies.

The lodge evoked a feeling difficult to capture in photographs or in memory. Slightly musty and dusty, it had the smell of a thousand fires kindled in the magnificent stone fireplace. There were cobwebs in places that could not be reached and an occasional bat in the rafters. There were memorable decorations, too —giant felt banners emblazoned with the camp name; countless panoramic pictures of campers and camp teams from seasons gone by; plaques, banners, and trophies from innumerable regattas, tournaments, and invitationals; stenciled Indian decorations on the beams; murals of camp life in the old days; and reminders of unforgettable performances by campers and counselors in a continuous chain from the early days till just last season.

Camp gathering places are generally crammed with mementos. At Camp Kennebec (upper left) banners from sailing, tennis, and swimming events festoon the rafters. At North Woods a mural from a long-ago nature hike adorns the camp playroom wall. The lodges at Wyonegonic—known as "wiggies" (short for wigwam)—are good places to sit around the fire in camp-designed wiggie chairs.

*This cozy cabin was adorned with a multitude of pennants and photos and even a throw rug for cold feet on chilly mornings.*

 # Living with Kids

Put a bunch of kids the same age in a cabin or a tent for a summer, with all their paraphernalia, and what did you get? Chaos.

Your group was as little as two campers in a small tent or as big as a gang of eight or more in a cabin with two counselors minding the peace. The living quarters almost always seemed cluttered, no matter what the size and population, partly because everyone was living out of a footlocker that ate up precious floor space. Even though all your gear arrived from home in your trunk (with bedding, shoes, and boots in a duffel), after the first day at camp you could never fit everything back in the way it came.

You were allowed to expand out of it to some degree (more clutter). Each person had an orange crate or some other improvisation by his or her bed, or a bona fide shelf unit. These were promptly filled up with books, comics, games, tissue boxes, baseballs, stationery, and baseball mitts. And then there was always the exposed two-by-four structure of the cabin itself— the perfect size for a can of tennis balls, a Brownie camera, and the latest postcard from home. In addition, there was the mess spilling out from under the bed: sneakers, spikes, oxfords, thongs, moccasins, boots, rubbers, baseball bats, and an occasional tennis racquet.

The walls in many cabins were plastered with camp and college pennants; pinups and posters of movie stars, recording stars, and athletes; and scrawled autographs from former residents. Anywhere an exposed nail had been pounded into the wall was a fair place to hang a cap, fins, goggles, belts, or a canteen.

Any space filled with as many trunks as beds, a jumble of mismatched dressers, and closets whose doors refused to stay shut was bound to be cramped, if not claustrophobic. In tents, where closet space was nonexistent, a broomstick, suspended with rope like a trapeze from the peak, *was* the closet.

Camp beds were a very special breed of furniture. They were always made with a heavy metal frame and had woven wire springs, which either sagged, hammock-fashion, or stretched with cruel boardlike rigidity. The mattresses, which generally crunched when you squeezed them, were of indeterminate age. Some camps decreed that beds be placed head to foot, "for reasons of health." But more often than not, the interior arrangements were decided upon by the inhabitants.

*Informal and formal bunk portraits—the top one likely to be found in a camper's scrapbook; the bottom one likely to be mailed home to the parents.*

*Off-beat bunk units at the Cheley Colorado Camps' Trail's End Ranch Camps—western camping, with a Wild West flavor. They may look unusual from the outside, but inside there was just a bunch of kids like anywhere else.*

*At most camps, cabins and tents were filled with campers' signatures and "I was here" scrawls. A solution at Camp Agawam was the putting up of bunk plaques designed by each cabin each summer and painted with the inhabitants' names. One in the shape of a tornado commemorated the most memorable event of that season. Lady Di also graced the wall the summer she became a princess.*

In the early days, tents were the only sleeping quarters, but at most camps cabins (called bungalows or bunks, depending on the local terminology) gradually replaced them, leading, in time, to the introduction of electricity and plumbing. In some camps electricity was even put in the *tents*. But diehards always fought the introduction of modern amenities. The bittersweet pill of camping was having to trek off to the bathrooms and showerhouses.

The central bathrooms at camp were an experience unto themselves. Back in the woods, behind the tent line, they were far enough away to make it a bit of a hike to reach them . . . but no one would have wanted them any closer. They were the sort of places where no one wanted to spend too much time, but if forced to you could always amuse yourself reading the graffiti, or adding to it. Many wooden stalls were punctuated by a few small holes, bored by an active penknife, but these usually were plugged with little wads of toilet paper. At boys' camps, the toilets were equipped with weighted wooden seats that stayed in an upright position unless held down. The older the facility, the stronger the aroma.

The naming of bathrooms at camps was pure folklore. House of Lords and House of Commons were popular terms at boys' camps (because there each man had his rightful seat). Greenies was the word at some girls' camps, because at one time the toilets were housed in green tents. Tebas came from T.B.'s, which was a reversal of B.T., standing for blue tents. The Perch, the Mountain House, the Waldorf-Astoria, and the Biltmore were among other euphemisms.

For the most part, if you weren't at an activity or a meal, chances were you'd be in your tent or cabin . . . or at least hanging around with your bunkmates. Add to that the forced time together—sleeping, cleanup, and rest hour—and you ended up spending a lot of time together . . . which was great if you all got along. Unfortunately, there was frequently one camper who didn't fit in. The goat.

There were a thousand reasons that someone didn't fit in, any one of which would have been enough to taunt a camper (if you were the taunting type). He or she might have been too fat or too thin, too short or too tall, a bad athlete, or a crybaby. Any erratic behavior was immediately recognized by bullies and used for ammunition.

Nicknaming, too, was a fact of life at camp. Sometimes the

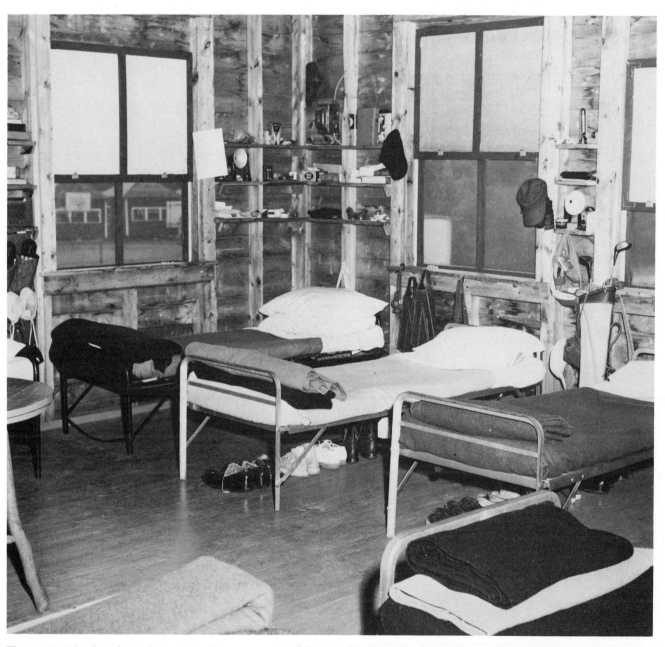

*The constant battle to keep clutter in its place was successfully waged in this cabin. It must be noted, though, that it took three days of straightening up to get this picture.*

*Some of the best times at camp were the hours spent lounging around in idle conversation. Invariably Brownie cameras appeared, and snapshots recorded the moments.*

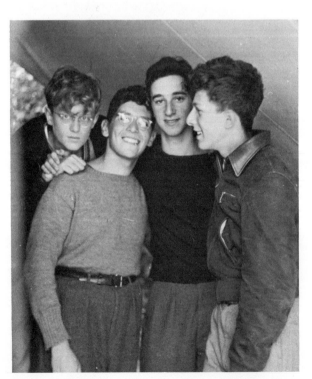

names were amusing and affectionate: Walter became Vulture; a heavy hitter was complimented with the name of Slugger. Others crossed that fine line between friendliness and mocking: The kid with the shortest crew-cut was known only as Skinhead, even long after his hair grew in.

There was once a fellow at camp who had the habit of always wearing an undershirt underneath a T-shirt, all summer long, no matter how hot the weather. Though ordinarily this wouldn't be remarkable, at camp this small fact could be blown out of all proportion. It wasn't long before he was known throughout camp only by the name Undershirt. A clever composer of camp ditties immortalized Undershirt in a song, often sung by the whole camp in the dining hall:

> *Undershirt, Undershirt, under an undershirt.*
> *He thinks he's grubby, he thinks he has lice,*
> *So he wears two shirts to protect himself twice.*

Despite the teasing, the clutter, and the little inconveniences, there were still some great things about living at camp for the summer. No parents! Even your counselor, the surrogate parent, was only a few years your senior. And he or she would do things your parents never would have, like bring you hamburgers in the wee hours—no matter if they were cold—on returning from a night off.

Of course, sharing a cabin with your friends all summer long was hard to beat. If you hadn't seen one another for ten months, you really had a lot to talk about. These whispered conversations could go on late into the night, until your counselor clamped down and put an end to them—for that night. Aside from going to activities, eating, and going on trips together—the organized camp routine—the friends in your cabin were also the ones with whom you could horse around, tell secrets, bet a nickel, and share comics and candy. When it came right down to it, a lot of camp was living with kids.

*Stuffed animals were favored camp take-alongs. A sign of true affection was letting a tentmate sleep with your animal. The menagerie here was on display for an animal show at Alford Lake Camp.*

*A group of Seniors in an unusually plush rustic cabin. At a full-season camp, by the time you were fifteen, you might have spent a year or more of summers living with your friends.*

*The lone bugler delivers the wake-up call.*

*If you wake up in the morning, and it's cold,*
*And you think the rising bell is awfully bold,*
*If you shiver like cold pups,*
*And you're late for setting-ups,*
*Laugh it off, oh camper, laugh it off!*

*If you're not so fond of oatmeal, laugh it off!*
*If your orange you can't peel, laugh it off!*
*If your breakfast you abhor,*
*And your bones feel awfully sore,*
*Laugh it off, oh camper, laugh it off!*

*If the bunk is just a sight, laugh it off!*
*If the corners won't lie right, laugh it off!*
*If you think that all is straight,*
*Yet you get no more than eight,*
*Laugh it off, oh camper, laugh it off!*

*Walden Camp Songs, 1926*

# Rise and Shine

Camp Tooth Brush.

"It's time to get up!" was the usual form of the rude awakening each cold morning at camp. Reveille was sometimes performed by an honest-to-goodness off-key and squeaky bugler; more often a scratchy, well-worn recording of the familiar tune, blasted over the loudspeaker, took its place. Camps with an aversion to the militaristic overtones of reveille would go to any means to substitute anything else. Classical music floating from the oaks at Douglas Ranch Camps or from the pines at Kehonka provided a gentler wake-up, some might say. A cheerful "Yoo Hoo" resounded through the bullhorn at Camp Walden every morning.

No matter how you were awakened, it was hard to get up. That chilly air tended to keep you firmly implanted in your toasty bed. There were always a *few* hardy souls who had no trouble jumping up, getting dressed, and facing the cold-water wash. The lazybones, on the other hand, were prodded, pulled, uncovered, and spritzed with water in attempts to extricate them from bed. The final recourse was to dump their mattresses to the floor of the tent or beyond, often with the counselor's help.

In the early days, it was mandatory to get up and dash off shivering to the lake in pajamas or swimsuit for setting-up exercises, "the usual torture of calisthenics." At Camp Winnebago they used to play calisthenic songs over the PA: "Okay, ready now, jumping jacks. And a one, two, one, two . . ." However, lakeside residents complained of the early morning noise, so the records were ended.

Typically, exercises were followed by a plunge in the lake, which, in its early morning calm, looked beautiful and deceptively inviting. Soaps, towels, and toothbrushes were all brought down, and the morning dip became the hurried daily wash.

We poor mortals [at Alford Lake Camp] climbed up to the camp house as usual for exercises, the wiser ones wearing two sweaters as it was very cold. The lake seemed almost heated when we jumped in for our dip, but when we came out the cold air turned us into little icebergs.

It's not hard to see why few campers enjoyed this method of getting the day started. In fact, the Girl Scouts came out against it in 1931, with the following manifesto:

The camping department of Girl Scouts is discouraging early morning setting-up exercises and prebreakfast dips. Eminent physicians advise

*The morning used to begin at the water's edge. Setting-up exercises (below) warmed your blood enough so that you might consider jumping in the lake. Ablutions (above) were the next order of business. If you'd forgotten your toothbrush, one could be fashioned quickly from a twig by fraying one end (top).*

33

*Salute the flag and hustle to the tables in the
tent,
Agate dishes sound as if they knew what it all
meant,
Even forty feet away the boys sometimes can
scent
    Good things to eat at Abnaki.
Hurrah! Hurrah! I'm hungry as a bear,
Hurrah! Hurrah! O see what's coming there;—
Waiter, tell the cook to give our table its full
share,
    Appetites are good at Abnaki.*

Camp Abnaki Handbook, *1921, to the tune of "Marching Through
Georgia."*

*Boys lined up on one side, girls on the other: Flag raising
could be very formal, even in the woods.*

*Inspection commanded another salute in a spotless tent in
the 1920s.*

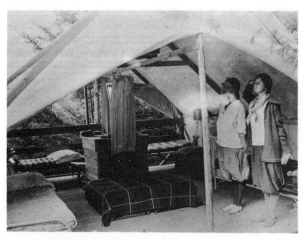

that human resistance is at its lowest ebb in the early morning. The nervous system may be injured by exercise taken on an empty stomach and the shock of cold water is devitalizing.

With the proliferation of showerhouses in camps, the morning rituals were done away with except on a voluntary basis. "Polar bear clubs" provided an excuse for anyone foolhardy enough to take a prebreakfast dip, and here machismo could be flaunted every morning, rain or shine.

En route to the dining hall, the camp gathered en masse to salute the rising flag to a bugle accompaniment, performed by the same incompetent bugler who woke you up earlier. Laggards who hadn't quite made it to the assembly froze in their tracks, removed their caps, and felt ever so slightly penitent for missing the event.

A dinner bell signaled the noisy onslaught of famished campers toward the breakfast table. No one wanted to be late for breakfast because the food was barely warm when you were on time. Camp breakfasts were notorious for, to quote a number of former campers, "pancakes that go boom!" sometimes "gelatinous oatmeal," "cold toast" on which butter refused to melt, "cold, watery scrambled eggs," and your choice of three-minute, five-minute, or ten-minute eggs, all of which were mysteriously done to the same degree. At the boys' camps rumors abounded that everything was laced with saltpeter.

On the other hand, there was always juice, hot chocolate every day, and all the sugar-coated cereal you could eat. One bunk at Camp Somerset in 1979 set about collecting their cereal boxes, and by the end of the season had amassed over six hundred.

Even if the food was hard to keep hot on the dining porch, it was almost always fresh. An early brochure glorifying camps in Maine boasted:

Milk, that highly important food for growing children, is delivered fresh from spotless dairies and is produced by herds that rank with the best in the world.

Maine hens are the healthiest in the world, a fact well-known to every poultryman. Eggs from Maine flocks are delivered to the camps just minutes from the time they are gathered.

After breakfast came the cacophony of morning announcements. Amid the clatter of dishes, the clinking of silverware, the banging of pots and pans, and the fidgeting of children, it is hard to imagine how anyone actually heard what was being said. Somehow the plan for the morning was passed along, and campers trooped back to their sleeping quarters. Sometimes a quick change of clothes was in order—shedding a sweater because the sun was a little higher, or trading sodden, dew-soaked sneakers for a new pair. Camp Fernwood used to require its girls to wear rubbers over sneakers every morning to flag raising because of the heavy dew.

Then some semblance of order had to be made of the bunks for daily inspection for the honor tent or honor cabin award. Your bed had to be meticulously made—hospital corners were a must—and all extra blankets were neatly piled at the foot of the bed. Your trunk, cupboard, and shelves had to be straightened up. Of course, all dirty clothing was confined to your laundry bag. After the floor was swept free of pine needles and dust, boots and shoes were lined up in pairs beneath the cot. Tent flaps were supposed to be rolled up neatly (from the inside), but were often just flung up onto the roof of the tent, and cabin shutters were raised by a system of frayed ropes and pulleys. Outside, litter had to picked up and the grounds raked.

As for inspection itself, it was usually highly contested, with the difference between winning and losing as little as a ball-point pen left on a bed. Occasionally accusations arose that campers whose cabins were inspected first ran ahead and distributed papers outside cabins still to be inspected, but this was atypical and certainly not within the spirit of cleanup and inspection.

Historically, the time between cleanup and first activity was devoted to camp improvement: rolling and sweeping the tennis courts, and scraping gypsy moth larvae off trees. This tradition descended from the early days of camping, when campers themselves actually cleared fields for baseball diamonds, constructed cabins, and even supplied wood for the cook's stoves and hauled ice from the icehouse for the refrigerators. Following local disasters, camp improvement always took on a new meaning. After the holocaust of 1930, when a major forest fire hit Camp Yawgoog, five hundred scouts planted twenty-five thousand seedlings. In 1974, a tornado wiped out two-hundred fifty pine trees at Camp Agawam in twenty minutes. For the rest of the summer, the camp improvement period was lengthened considerably, as campers hauled brush and prepared the trees for a local mill to come in and saw up the wood.

When camp was shipshape, the activities started and the fun began.

A COUNCILOR's TASK IS RATHER MEAN :
TO KEEP THE CAMPERS GAY AND CLEAN !

*An Androscoggin counselor portrayed one of his duties, when personal inspection was part of the daily routine.*

*Unalayee campers teamed up to clear the grounds in a heavy-duty camp improvement program.*

*The Junior baseball team poses for a picture in 1937, surrounding a precariously constructed centerpiece at home plate.*

*Hey, batter! Hey, batter! . . . Softball in 1955.*

# Fields, Diamonds, and Courts

"On occasion the whole camp takes to the water and sweeps down the length of the lake, seven miles, to play ball with a rival team at Denmark." As early as 1910, the Winona Camps' third season, playing against other camps was a major event. After seven miles of paddling, though, it probably wasn't much of a contest.

As soon as you got to camp, making the teams of your choice was a high priority. If you were good at sports, this was no problem; others had to work a bit harder to achieve their aims. It was easy to finagle your way onto the softball team. (After all, nine played at a time.) One camper recalled making his father buy him a first baseman's glove, figuring no one else might have one, and he'd have the position sewed up—which he did. Other campers arrived loaded with catcher's gear, because that was one position few wanted to play.

Part of the fun of being on a team was getting to go to other camps. Beyond the excitement of the contest itself, there was the possibility of seeing friends from home who went to the other camps. Anyway, it was always a treat to be able to leave camp and come back with stories to tell. A Winona camper from the 1940s recalled another benefit. Any time his camp traveled to Wigwam for a game, everyone wanted to go because the food was so great over there. And there was always the chance that there'd be a social to look forward to after the game.

But even if you made the trip, that didn't mean you'd see much action, in the game or afterward:

Dear Mom & Dad, On Wednesday night I went to Indian Acres for a baseball game (16 & under) and a dance. I didn't play and the dance was lousy. There were no girls my size.

Up through the 1940s, barnstorming teams crisscrossed the countryside in well-worn school buses and rattletrap open-bodied trucks with canvas tops and roll-down sides. Inside would be crammed one or more camp teams with the requisite counselors/coaches/chaperones. These traveling players would descend on a different camp each day for a match-up, a meal or two, and an overnight stay. Several cabins' worth of campers, at the host's camp, were displaced by shuffling them into beds vacated by kids on trips or in the infirmary. In the morning the visitors would take their leave and move on to the next camp. After four or five days on the road, several hotly contested bat-

*At bat on the lower diamond.*

37

*Three lefties learning the toss at tennis instruction. Southpaws were often lumped together.*

*Practicing at Kennebec for the Invitation Meet in 1933.*

tles, countless ice-cream cone interruptions, one evening at the movies, a requisite dance, and five hundred miles under their belts, the campers would straggle into camp, happy, tired, and hungry.

Barnstorming was usually left to the older campers. The little kids had enough trouble playing one game at a stretch. *Bean Soup* from 1979, Camp Pemigewassett's log, described a typical slaughter:

### TEN AND UNDER BASEBALL

On the way to the Moose, the team's confidence was overflowing. The coaches had planned their strategy: which consisted of blowing out the Moosilauke team and utilizing the bench early. Unfortunately, we don't always get what we want, and the final score was a lopsided total of 27–0. The team fought bravely to the end, but the game was halted in the third inning just as we were making a comeback. Maybe next time we will get a chance to play the full six innings.

Some intercamp competitions have always carried much more prestige than others, and the pressure under which you had to perform could be very intense. The Kennebec Invitation Tennis Meet was started in 1914 and continues today. It has been described in recent years as "formal and ceremonious," with a "Wimbledon-like hush." Bleachers were moved to court-side from the baseball diamond, and paying spectators sat in tents bordering the courts.

A Wigwammer in this esteemed tournament during the late 1940s recalled a more vocal, highly charged atmosphere. Strong in his memory was the feeling of having two hundred keyed-up Kennebec campers cheering for his opponent and eight people representing his camp contingency cheering for him. He also recalled his winning strategy. The distance from the baseline back to the fence was rather short, so he perfected his top spin lob all season to use at Kennebec.

While a lucky few were competing for coveted berths in the big tournaments, the rest of the campers were enjoying camp life at a more leisurely pace: slapping balls up against the back-board, trying to keep them from disappearing into the woods beyond; dribbling basketballs and soccer balls; shagging flies in the blistering outfield while dreaming of bug juice; and learning to unscramble a hopeless rotation on the volleyball court.

*No spikers amid this motley crew.*

### SOCCER

What is this noise of a whistle, the shouts of "Play your position!" "Ouch, my toe"? Soccer is in progress. It is a famous old English game, sometimes called Rugby football and played by both men and women. To a spectator it might look like a mob of twenty on top of the ball, but we hope by the middle of the summer we will be playing real, fast, clean games. Just at present the old kicking instinct is predominant and elbows jab and poke with much gusto. Soccer is an excellent game because even unskilled players can get real enjoyment out of it; it does not require a very even field; the equipment is relatively inexpensive; and it requires the use of muscles which are not exercised in our everyday sedentary life. We hope that every girl will like and play soccer well by the end of the summer—then it will be soccer, not "sock-her."

*Soccer was relatively unknown when introduced to Camp Somerset in 1928. Now no camp could do without it. From Somer = Settings, volume 1, number 2.*

*Basketball in bloomers could draw quite a crowd.*

The founder of WoHeLo, with her three daughters, kindled the flame with rubbing sticks. All council fires since 1909 have been started there in this fashion—getting things off in true Indian style.

# Indian Lore

The distant beat of the tom-tom alerted you to gather your blankets and feathers and file into the council ring. The weekly council fire was an eagerly anticipated event. Its mysteries, drama, excitement, and spirituality mingled to create an unforgettable camp experience.

The magic of lighting the fire set the tone for the evening. There were countless ways this was accomplished. The fire might, after appropriate songs and chanting, miraculously light itself. A flaming arrow might touch it off, as was done at Indian Acres. At Camp Buckskin for Boys, after the chief had called plaintively to the four winds, the "fire god," carrying a torch, would whoop in from the woods like a wild Indian.

The only problem with the fire lighting itself was that it didn't always work. A camper from the thirties at Kennebec Junior recalled a near miss. The flame, when called upon, raced along the ground from the woods and got within ten feet of the piled wood when it expired. The chief, without missing a beat, announced, "Tonight we light the fire in the manner of the white man." Whereupon a cigarette lighter did the honors.

After the fire had been kindled, awards of the week were announced, for which campers, sometimes known only as braves and often regaled in Indian headdresses, received feathers, candles, felt patches, or other symbols of honor in a sacred, carefully orchestrated ceremony. The young Indians would then dance in a circle around the fire, being careful *not* to do the rain dance. Challenges, contests, charades, and singing rounded out the night.

"The chief" was usually another name for the camp director. But sometimes council fire was led by the camp Indian. Summer camps across the country provided part-time employment for Indians who headed up Indian lore programs.

In the 1930s, Ralph Allen, a.k.a. Lone Bear, began a thirty-year summer career as a resident Indian. Lone Bear was a full-blooded Pawnee, whose grandfather was Chief White Eagle, last hereditary chief of the Pawnee tribe. In the off-season, he was an actor, singer, and model who'd graduated from the Juilliard School of Music. At camp, Lone Bear taught basketry and Indian lore, organized an Indian club, conducted council fire, and helped out in archery—the traditional activities of the camp Indian.

The youngest campers were often crazy about the camp Indian and his games and stories. They tagged along with him whenever possible, and their enthusiasm sparked him to retell

*The little chief's headdress appears twice the size of that of the resident Indian at Camp Lilliput.*

*Frequently a tepee such as this was the official headquarters of the Indian lore program at camp.*

41

Campers here have mixed their metaphors. The young
braves use nautical signals while donning Indian costume.

native legends, myths, chants, and dances, to their amazement
and awe.

One Indian custom carried on by campers was the decora-
tion of canoe paddles. For the Indians, the paddle was a symbol
of exploration, and many adventures were recorded in paint on
the blades. Indians decorated paddles to make them accomplish
their jobs more effectively—eyes might be painted on a paddle,
in order that it might avoid hidden rocks. A fish or other symbol
of speed would help the canoe move swiftly. Translated into
camp life, any abstraction of an Indian symbol might do. Tepees,
tomahawks, and peace pipes were crudely represented in oils
and covered with sloppily applied coats of varnish on hurried
artists' paddles. Those more serious—and more artistic—re-
garded their paddles as potential masterpieces, and spent many
hours on the design and execution. These personalized paddles
became the campers' property, to be shlepped home for the
winter and back to camp year after year.

Camp was permeated with the influence of the Indian—if
not in the form of a person of Indian heritage, who strutted
around camp in a loincloth and headdress, then in its language
and activities. Many camps had Indian names. The main building was the lodge; a tepee usually sat by the lake; you paddled
around in Indian canoes, made beaded belts, moccasins, and
baskets; and paid homage to the totem poles around the camp.
Even if there wasn't an out-and-out Indian lore program, you
lived in the shadow of the red man.

But when there was a structured program, the emotional
climax was without a doubt the ghost rock ceremony. During
the last week of camp, each camper and counselor found a
stone small enough to carry in one hand (how easily carried was
another matter). It was painted up with his or her name, team,
and year, and anything else that could be squeezed on it. At the
final council fire, the stones were solemnly, tearfully, and cere-
moniously laid along the path to the council ring. Together they
represented the camp family as a group that would spiritually
stay together long after they'd gone their separate ways.

The spirits of former campers and counselors at Camp Agawam live on in their ghost rocks—left by the trail to the council ring.

The original Camp Fire Girls at WoHeLo stand proudly in formation. Paddles were awarded for achieving first canoeing and swimming honors. The girls then embellished them with elaborate painted decorations.

*The bird watchers compare notes and nests of their feathered friends.*

# Let Nature Take Its Course

Like poison ivy, nature was avoided at camp. Few campers derived genuine joy from the subject of nature. Most would later brag that in all their years at camp they never set foot in the nature lodge. If not an outright lie, these claims were surely exaggerations. After all, when you were in the youngest group of campers you *had* to go to nature. And you probably liked it too. But nature had stiff competition. The sedentary life of bug and leaf collecting was no match for tennis, baseball, riflery, and water-skiing.

Some kids actually liked to scour the woods and fields, day in and day out, to build their rock, mushroom, and butterfly collections into true wonders. But most couldn't be bothered to work such activities into their precious schedules.

Most kids felt nature meant learning lists—and that was too reminiscent of school days. As Cap'n Bill Vinal, renowned naturalist, put it in 1932: "The camper can still earn medals and insignia with 'lists.' He chants the 'bird list,' for example, and an emblem is sewed onto the proper place. Then the 'bird list' is promptly forgotten because the camper must pass on to the 'bug list.'"

The problem with nature was that it had a bad rep. First and foremost was the misconception that only wimps did nature. Therefore a jock wouldn't be caught dead there . . . under penalty of being held up to ridicule by other sports fiends. On the next level, this attitude sifted down to those who wished they were better athletes than they were. Likewise, they couldn't patronize the nature lodge because that would be admitting defeat on the sports field. So there you had it: 85 percent of the camp population was ruled out of ever doing nature.

All in all, the nature counselor had quite an uphill battle to fight. One drawing card he used with great success was having live animals around camp. Forlorn campers, homesick for their pets, flocked around the "wild" animals that needed to be fed and looked after. A family of half-grown skunks, known affectionately as "wood pussies," were often the surrogate felines in camp. A couple of hens and roosters fascinated the midget campers all summer, and a billy goat, usually named Billy the Kid, with its mischief and pranks, was often popular. One camp even had a temperamental miniature bucking burro that had been in a circus.

For the budding naturalists inclined to head for the nature shack, more was in store for them than dead bugs and dried

*Eight animal skins adorn the entrance to a nature lodge. All of the animals were found dead near camp, killed by cars or neighboring cats. They include two foxes and two weasel skins.*

45

*Learning about aquatic life with the feet-in, hands-on approach.*

leaves. Life teemed in camp beehives specially harbored there, and honey in the comb was worth the chance of a sting. The bird watchers in the group could do some real field work by banding whatever they could catch. In 1924, the lads at Greylock proudly reported that they had managed to band seven birds during the summer, including one hard-to-catch ovenbird. There were also perks for the stargazers: bathrobe lessons in astronomy every clear night between tattoo and taps. Or you could learn to approach a groundhog, Indian-style, by crawling toward it on your stomach until it spied you and disappeared down a hole. Other campers wandered the woods, looking for the wonders of nature, and were rewarded with glimpses of great blue herons feeding, muskrats swimming, and bobcats turning tail and darting away.

Nowadays, nature has been renamed ecology or environmental studies. Closely linked to "fun" activities, such as hiking and no-trace camping, kids get a healthy dose of nature and practically don't even realize it.

At Camp Unalayee in California, they recently inaugurated a new "environmental forum," where campers hiked through the Trinity Alps for eight days. They were met along the route by guest speakers, who seemed to appear out of nowhere to hike with them while sharing some of their expertise. A geologist explained volcanic action. An entomologist caught bugs and described their life cycles. All of this was a far cry from the traditional nature lodge at camp, with its moldy specimens from God-knows-when, its bug-eaten leaf collections, and sun-faded cut-outs from old *Life* magazines and *National Geographic*s.

The standard fixture, though, that you could count on in almost any camp—whether it had a great nature program or a nearly nonexistent one—was the nature trail. It was sometimes hacked out of the woods by an energetic group of campers and counselors insistent upon spreading the gospel. Crudely painted signs with the barest minimum of information were placed at strategic points. Other times the nature trail was set up by a visiting naturalist, hired to inject a new level of nature enthusiasm into the camp population at large. At its worst, the trail provided the camper with a good excuse for a walk in the woods; at its best, a bit of education in a pleasant atmosphere. The tree walk at Camp Pemigewassett consisted of twenty-seven trees located throughout the camp. Each carried a sign like No. 13:

*Animals at camp, no matter what they are, are always a favorite. Old-time Watitoh campers were fascinated by a young billy goat (left), while a porcupine, raccoon, and falcon made friends with a nature counselor (right).*

*Inside the nature lodge at Camp Pemigewassett, butterflies decorate the walls, and ferns for studying grow right outside.*

*Emerging from the nature trail with specimens in hand and tales of those that got away.*

🌲 🌲 🌲 🌲 🌲 🌲 🌲 🌲 🌲 🌲 🌲 🌲 🌲 🌲 🌲

### BEECH [*Fagus grandifolia*]

It is said that a beech tree is never struck by lightning, and that a man can seek refuge under it in a thunder storm with absolute safety.

Notice the thin papery leaves with prominent veins on the underside running parallel to each other and at an angle of 45 degrees from the midvein. Notice, too, the smooth gray bark.

It has the kind of bark that tempts a boy with a knife to carve his initials in it. Our word *book* comes from the Anglo-Saxon *boc,* meaning a letter or a character, which in turn derives from an earlier Anglo-Saxon word *beece,* meaning the beech tree. No doubt characters inscribed on the trunks of ancient trees were the first books. It is this tree, in all probability, that Shakespeare had in mind in *As You Like It:*

> O Rosalind! These trees shall be my books,
> And in their bark my thoughts I'll character,
> That every eye that in this forest looks
> Shall see thy virtue witnessed everywhere.

An ancient beech tree which fell in Washington County, Tennessee, in 1916, for years bore this inscription on its bark:

> D. Boone
> Killed a Bar
> On Tree
> In Year 1760

Thus explorers, though often unlettered, could record events on the bark of such trees. Others passing by would know that it was Daniel Boone who killed a bear there. The Daniel Boone tree, when it fell, was estimated by the count of its annual rings to have been 365 years old. Therefore it began to grow in the year 1551, half a century before Shakespeare wrote the lines in *As You Like It.*

The nuts are eagerly sought by squirrels and chipmunks. They often forget where they store them, thus, the next spring these forgotten nuts begin to sprout, and we must credit Mother Nature with another method of seed dispersal.

There are two three-sided nuts in each bur. After the frost, they ripen and may be gathered. They are sweet and good to eat. Farmers used them along with acorns to fatten their hogs. They called such food mast.

The wood makes excellent fuel, and is occasionally used in the manufacture of chairs, tool handles, plane stocks, shoe last and similar articles.

NO. 14 IS THE RED PINE ON THE RIGHT SIDE OF THE ROAD JUST THIS SIDE OF THE BASKETBALL COURT.

🌲 🌲 🌲 🌲 🌲 🌲 🌲 🌲 🌲 🌲 🌲 🌲 🌲 🌲 🌲

Unassuming as it may seem, this nature lodge was set up in the early twenties by Dr. Clyde Fisher, curator of the American Museum of Natural History in New York, during one of his many summers as head nature counselor.

The nature department commandeers a fleet of boats for a specimen-gathering trip up Mutiny Brook in 1924.

*Last one in is a rotten egg.*

*Bathing beauties lounging in the sun.*

# Buddy Up!

Sinkers, minnows, bass, pickerel, and salmon. Tadpoles, perch, tortoises, frogs, and frogmen. Classification at the waterfront! Campers nationwide were known as species of sea life, depending on their levels of fearlessness and skill. A Kennebec camper from 1952 wrote home, "Dear Mom and Dad, I caught a bass and a white perch. I am a 4 and a ½ part bass in swimming. . . . Love and x x."

Testing your water abilities and amassing Red Cross badges were always a high priority. Soon after arrival all campers were marched down to the lake to prove themselves. The nonswimmers were confined to the "crib," an ignominious area, waist-deep (for even the smallest camper) and bordered by docks. Docks forming H-shapes, L-shapes, U-shapes, T-shapes . . . each could be found, along with rope and buoys, defining the area in which you were allowed to swim. Woe to any camper who strayed beyond! Floats, rafts, springboards, towers, and chutes added to the clutter of the waterfront, intruding on the view of the lake.

"Fine, sandy beaches," "spring-fed lakes, small enough to be safe, large enough to be fun!" were touted in many camp brochures. (Of course, not all camps were located on lakes. An occasional camp was on a river or at the ocean, and others even had pools.)

Swim instruction was required of everyone. This in itself could have filled up the day for that dictator known as the waterfront director, but he or she also had to fit in your free-swim periods, swim team practices for all age groups, swim meets, life-saving instruction, and diving lessons. It goes without saying that the waterfront director may have been the only person in camp who prayed for rainy days.

The first goal of every camper was to be certified safe in deep water, because only after that could you participate in water sports, such as sailing, canoeing, and water-skiing. The standard ordeal was to survive the thirty-minute test, in which you had to swim, tread water, float, or otherwise remain in water over your head for half an hour. Only after this could you swim beyond the crib. From that point on, you couldn't be bothered with the sinkers left splashing behind in the crib.

For nonswimmers it was another matter. To even be classified as a tadpole, you had to first walk out in water to the crosswalk, no mean feat for a petrified youngster. Then you actually had to put your face in the water!; duck under the sur-

*Practicing the flutter kick while keeping the water out of the nose.*

*Swimming milestones were regularly reported to parents.*

51

The buddy system reigned supreme at the waterfront. It could be used with a board and tag system, such as the one at Camp Lenox, where swimmers chose their buddies and indicated they were in the water by moving a numbered marker on the board. At the whistle and command, "Buddy up!" partners swam to each other and kept clasped hands raised. They counted off while the counselor made the count from dockside.

The well-known life-saving jump was practiced on four would-be victims awaiting their rescue.

*The waterfront apparatus as it used to be in the teens at Camp Kehonka.*

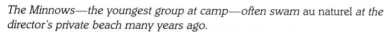

*The Minnows—the youngest group at camp—often swam au naturel at the director's private beach many years ago.*

*Working toward a life-saving badge—the cross-chest carry.*

A near-perfect jackknife at a Camp Kennebec swim meet.

"We won! We won!"

face for six seconds—*with* your eyes open; push and glide for five feet—*with* your face in the water; and finally swim with water wings for twenty-five yards.

The more ambitious campers naturally tried to advance up the aquatic ladder, collecting wallet-size certificates for each new level attained. Subsequent skills included thirty-two minutes of continuous swim, four minutes of each stroke; flip turns; deep dives to a depth of twenty-five feet; and underwater swim for thirty yards.

Most girls' camps stressed swimming for form rather than water stunts. At Tripp Lake Camp, different colored bathing caps indicated swimming ability and technique. Most prestige came with the white cap, so difficult to attain that sometimes only a single camper would make it in a season.

For the avid waterdog, going out for the camp swim team was always an option and brought with it the fierce competition of swim meets. Here the camper had the chance to travel to other camps—which, if far enough away, could mean an overnight at a motel. An invitational at Camp Belgrade in 1961 included lunch at the host camp for all the visiting teams—which was often reason enough to try to make the trip. Following the meet was a stop for dinner at a Lobster Pound restaurant (for something you *rarely* got at camp) and a short stop for a half-hour stretch to bowl a string of duckpins at a local alley.

It was always a novelty to participate in a swim meet at a camp on a river, such as Indian Acres. In races of two laps or more, the split times were hilarious. Starting out with the current, you could make the first twenty-five yards in ten seconds or less; coming back, you'd be lucky to break thirty.

The price you paid to be on the swim team, however, was a dear one. Without a doubt, the practices were the most agonizing of any team at camp: day after day of hours in the water swimming laps and sprints, on sunny days and gray days, hot days and cold days, staying in until you shivered in spasms and your lips turned blue.

One problem every camp faced was the child who wouldn't go near the water. Some were great athletes on the tennis court or baseball diamond, but just didn't like to swim. Others were plainly terrified. They turned to devious methods in order to stay out of the water. The standard teenage girls' excuse was feigning illness or cramps more than once a month. But a mean waterfront director at Camp Hiawatha would keep a mental record of all girls. She knew after their first period when they couldn't possibly have cramps again.

Some children would revert to anything to avoid putting their faces in the water. There was always the excuse (invariably a fabrication) that "My mom says I don't have to go in." Others pointed tearfully to bandaged wounds, also usually without success. Some even claimed that the family doctor wouldn't approve, as in this lament from a camp director during the 1920s:

Goggles wears his great thick-rimmed glasses down to morning dip. He seldom goes in further than waist-deep. Our one, lone non-swimmer, he taxes the counselor patience and I believe he'd be thrown in off the dock if I would allow it. Stands on the shore arguing the relative dangers of staying dirty or catching cold by going into the water out of the sun. Holds a brief for hot-water against dirt and complains because camp has no bath-tub. Says he needn't learn to swim because his eyes are too weak—couldn't avoid dangers because he'd not see them! Must wear his glasses as doctor so instructed—never be without them! . . . Funny little old-man, Goggles.

The natural beauty of swimming in a lake was just not enjoyed by some campers who got the creeps from muddy bottoms, swimming with fishes and an occasional water snake, leech, or eel. One camper from Catawba claimed twenty years later that he still couldn't swim in a lake with a mud bottom after several summers spent at the Camp Catawba swimming hole.

For campers who liked nothing better than a plunge in the lake, one of the favorite swim events was the skinny-dip. This occurred in every camp, whether organized or illicit. At Tevya, in the 1950s, there was a weekly skinny-dip on Friday afternoons for both the boys' and girls' camps . . . at their separate beaches. One former camper surmised this was merely a ploy to get everyone in camp clean before the Friday night services. He also remarked that the boys *always* thought the girls were spying on them, and vice versa.

Throughout the summer, so much time was spent down at the lake, lying on the sand, building castles, sunning on a raft, sitting on the docks, floating on a paddleboard, swimming laps, splashing in the water, or taking lessons. It's really hard to believe that some kids actually made it through camp without learning how to swim.

*Practicing breathing to the side in the crib.*

IF YOU'RE ANXIOUS FOR TO SHINE
*(To a tune by Gilbert and Sullivan; words by Miriam and Auguste Spectorsky)*

*If you're anxious for to shine
In the deep aquatic line
As a girl of prowess rare,
You must plunge in very early,
With a manner far from surly
Come up smiling for your air.
You must lie upon the water
Just like Daddy Neptune's daughter,
Keep flopping in a fish-like way.
You must wriggle to the bottom,
Look for pearls and when you've got 'em,
Come up smiling bright and gay.*

*Echoes of Lenore Songs of 1931.*

*Lazing on a paddleboard was a good way to pass the time . . . and get a sunburn.*

*The lunge and parry at fencing instruction in 1936 at Greylock.*

# Sports That Say "Camp"

The "crack" of the rifle, the "twang" of the bowstring, and the "thunk" of the arrow hitting the straw target were heard in the backwoods of camp, far from the buzz of activity. Archery, riflery, fencing, and boxing were somehow in a different league from the "big" camp team sports.

Nearly every kid tried riflery at camp. The idea of "playing" with real guns was irresistible. But all campers soon found out that there was no "playing" to be done on the rifle range. The riflery counselor was even more strict than the waterfront counselor, if that was possible. Any horsing around and you were out instantly. No ifs, ands, or buts.

If you were serious about riflery, you spent a lot of time and a lot of ammunition down at the range. You got very accustomed to the smell of gunpowder mixed with the musty smell of the mattress on which you'd lie, which mingled with the aroma of the pine woods that surrounded you. You quickly learned the basic routine. The first problem was setting up your target—attaching it to a beaverboard backing to reel out to the end of the range. Unfortunately, most of the beaverboard was shot away, so it could be quite difficult. And if you didn't press those thumbtacks in hard enough, your target might flutter away in the middle of a round, forcing everyone to unload their guns, while you trekked out to the no-man's-land of the range to re-affix your target.

After the intense concentration of shooting a round, you reeled in your target to add up your score—always hoping for that "wallet shot," the bull's-eye so perfect you could cut it out and carry it around for show.

Similar concentration was going on at the archery range. Novices were known for their chafed forearms and sore fingers, in addition to the long walks they took in the woods searching for arrows that missed not only the mark, but also the backstop. You could tell the experts before they even started shooting— by how incredibly far back their targets were set.

The archery shack itself, from which all equipment was dispensed, was a place of great mystery. No larger than a tollbooth, entered *only* by the counselor and always locked up, it seemed to have a perpetual supply of bows and arrows, but never enough leather forearm shields and two-fingered gloves. From its small porch, the counselor took charge, bellowing commands: "Archers, nock your arrows! Commence firing!"

*Steadying the bow and taking aim for a photograph in 1938. In actual fact, the boys in front would definitely be behind the archers.*

*Learning to shoot in the prone position is the easiest way of all, but try telling that to a new camper.*

The balance beam and parallel bars are standard apparatus at most camps today. Not long ago, gymnastics was known as tumbling or acrobatics.

Many learned golf for the first time at camp, either on camp-owned golf courses or municipal links.

The Robin Hood romance that was tamed on the archery range also inspired young would-be swordplayers to try a hand at fencing, a sport that was difficult to find anywhere other than camp. Unfortunately, when suited up in all the protective gear on a hot day, the romance fizzled quickly. Not only that, those drills were really hard, and fencing turned out to be a sport that few kids stuck with.

Surprisingly enough, boxing is an offspring of fencing, where every lead and parry is taken from a similar attack and parry in fencing. Boxing was, for many years, very popular in many boys' camps, both as a sport and for resolving grudges. A *Kohut Kronikles* from 1927 described the action as "not slugging fights but fast scientific battles." Like other sports, instruction in boxing was taken as an activity, and the boys often got to perform in the ring in front of the whole camp as an evening program.

Whereas boxing, once commonplace, is seldom seen today, some camp sports never died. Waiting for your turn of "winners" at the Ping-Pong table was definitely a part of camp. The horrible conditions always made it more of a challenge. You were lucky to find a ball that was undented or a paddle with its rubber surface still intact. And, of course, the uneven, dim lighting made it even harder to hit the ball. The table's edge handicapped you further, as incoming balls skidded unpredictably off the eroded wood—chipped away by countless frustrated smashes of the paddle after missed shots.

As a classic way to bide your time, Ping-Pong in the lodge before dinner was only equaled by the all-time camp activities of quoits and horseshoes afterward.

*Landing punches at boxing class—a pair of six-year-olds at Camp Arcadia in 1948.*

*Measuring for the point at a close game of quoits in 1954.*

*Walking in the ring is where it all starts for the beginners.*

# Saddled Up

During the summers from 1916 to 1920, the daughter of the manager of the horses for Barnum and Bailey Circus went to Camp Arcadia. So for those seasons Arcadia had no trouble getting horses for their riding program. No trouble, that is, if you don't consider counselors taking the train to Portland in two shifts to pick up the thirty-five horses and riding them back thirty miles to camp before the season, and repeating the effort in the other direction at the end of the season any trouble.

The problem with horseback riding was that it was often considered an "extra," which meant that it cost more. If you couldn't convince your parents to shell out for it, you couldn't join your friends on the trails. Some former campers have remained unhappy about this "deprivation" more than twenty-five years after the fact.

The riding programs in camp ran the full gamut: learning to approach a horse ten times bigger than yourself, caring for horses and tack, jumping, dressage, English and Western riding, trail rides, pack trips, and vaulting (acrobatics on horseback). Some camps started off beginners with vaulting, which was done on a lunge line, in the ring, with the horse saddled with a special blanket with handles. The horse walked very slowly and the camper mounted with the horse in motion. While concentrating very hard on doing a somersault or other gymnastic feat without falling off, fear of being on a horse just disappeared.

Once you were comfortable on the horse, you concentrated on riding for show and racking up ribbons or hitting the trails in true cowboy fashion.

A 1943 article by Portia Mansfield of the Perry-Mansfield Camps in *The Camping Magazine* listed essential articles for girls to take on a pack trip: a ten-gallon hat was a must, for shade and to fill full of oats for the horse to eat; long-legged underwear to keep the creases of your blue jeans from chafing the skin; gloves for protection from the blistering sun, which could cause permanent skin blotches; a bandanna, described as so useful no reasons need be given for its inclusion; and for your pocket, pomade lipstick, a few pieces of dried fruit, peppermint candy, some string, tissues, and a scout knife. Last, a long-sleeved boy's woolen shirt (cooler than cotton in hot weather), "to tie around the waist by its sleeves if you are lucky enough to be in far-away country where one can ride 'a la nature' from belt line up (twenty minutes out of each hour should be maximum for even those accustomed to the sun)."

*Out for a trail ride in the Rocky Mountains at the Cheley Colorado Camps.*

61

*Saddling up the packhorse for an overnight.*

For pack trips or horse shows, beginners or experts, camp was a great place to learn about riding and to hang around horses. Many summer love affairs blossomed in the stables. A Somerset camper from 1930 penned these words:

I gathered her in my arms. What beautiful big, brown eyes she had! Like pools of the deep! And her lips, how delicate, but yet how firmly shaped! Her skin was like that of a new-born babe. I held her head high up for all campers to see—Nellie, the horse I was riding.

*A class of ten Wyonegonic campers on horseback, under the watchful eye of the riding master, near Pleasant Mountain in Maine, in the thirties.*

*Girls in love with horses make up a sizable majority of every camp that has riding. Three girls in saddle shoes await their turns.*

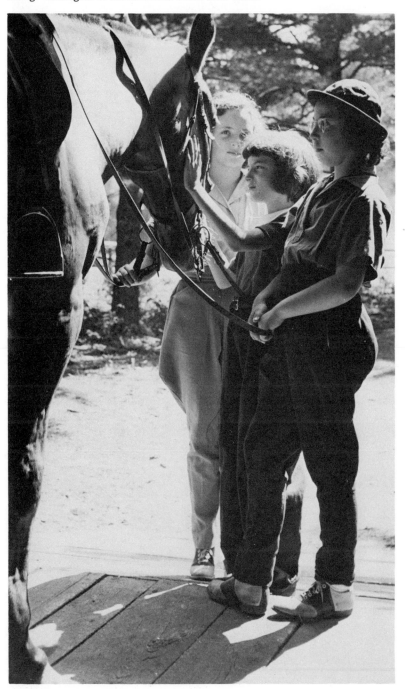

*Taking a jump—a determined camper at Wicosuta perfects her skills, 1973.*

*A Tapawingo camper leads a trail ride, English style, in the woods of Maine.*

*Dining hall din is dissipated when tables are spread out the length of the porch.*

# Mealtime

Most kids didn't like camp food—which didn't necessarily mean that the food was bad. It just had achieved a certain notoriety. You went to camp expecting not to like the food. This, despite claims on the excellence of the camp "table" in brochures. "The food is wholesome and well prepared and is a feature of the camp. Chocolate is served for breakfast, certified milk at noon, and a fruit drink for supper."

It seems that the camp menu was always "scientifically prepared" by a "trained dietician." (This may have had something to do with it not tasting like mom's cooking. It was also a function of cooking for hundreds of people at a time.) In the early days, it was always important to stress the freshness of all the food and its ample supply. "At two meals each day boys are allowed all the pasteurized milk they can drink, which is sometimes as much as eight glasses." This was nothing compared to how much a boy could drink if he was really thirsty. One camper bragged to his parents in a postcard home from 1951: "I am having a great time. I had 13 Glasses of punch during the 4'th of July celebration."

The items always gobbled up were the bakers' specialties: "From the Waldemar bakery come the homemade biscuits, hot rolls, pies, cookies, and birthday cakes, which make every camper a hungry camper." Who wasn't hungry for goodies like those? "The girl who 'just won't eat' at home sends back for 'seconds' at Waldemar and often begs Mother to secure the recipe for such Waldemar specialties as honey-nut rolls or chocolate sundae pie." Other camps had their own long-standing traditions, usually on Sunday mornings: homemade schnecken at Walden and homemade doughnuts at Lenore-Owaissa and North Woods.

The day-to-day fare, though, was not always so popular. It may have sounded good when you heard the menu, but the reality didn't always live up to expectations. Spaghetti and meatballs would generally be a crowd pleaser. But if it was cook's night off, and an incompetent boiled the spaghetti, you may have been expected to eat a congealed mass of rubberized pasta. On the other hand, one outstanding meal may have been a trade-off for several marginal ones. A sample week's entrees for dinner (which was at noon) in 1934 included roast chicken, lamb chops, ham, meat loaf, egg dish, sliced fish, and potted beef. Unfortunately, supper was then treated as an afterthought. Some of the bizarre combinations were cold cereal, cheese

### Morning
*Gracious Giver of all good,*
*Thee we thank for rest and food.*
*Grant that all we do or say*
*In Thy service be this day.*

### Noon
*Father for this noonday meal*
*We would speak the praise we feel,*
*Health and strength we have from Thee,*
*Help us, Lord, to faithful be.*

### Night
*Tireless guardian of our way,*
*Thou hast kept us well this day.*
*While we thank Thee, we request*
*Care continued, pardon, rest.*
*—Camp Wawayanda*

These graces appeared in a camping book in 1911 and are still sung at many camps.

The back cover of a folding "camp note" gave a quick summary of what was happening at camp. This camper elaborated in a later postcard. "Food is horrid! Horrid! Horrid!!!!!"

A group of scouts at Camp Yawgoog chow down on some lunch.

A late night trip back to the dining hall for a birthday party finds campers in pj's.

dreams with bacon, Waldorf salad, and a jelly roll; seedless grapes, pineapple juice, baked beans, and plain lettuce; and heated Rice Krispies cereal, parsley omelet, a few string beans, and a gelatin dessert.

For those who just couldn't manage to force down what was offered, even when holding their breath, there was a perpetual supply of peanut butter and jelly (or marshmallow fluff). One camp, Wihakowi, went so far as to rule, on their 1929 application form, that the girl "must not find fault with the food nor criticize same, except to the Dietician." Other camps had a better sense of humor regarding the fare; Camp Pemigewassett, for example, mentioned in its 1950s brochure: "In our more than forty years there has been no complaint regarding the food except that most boys don't like scrambled eggs." Camp Ousamequin didn't necessarily mean to be funny when it wrote: "After twelve years, all we need to say about the food at Ousamequin is that it is varied and ample"—which wasn't saying much.

When you elbowed your way into the dining hall, you headed right for your table, which you shared with your bunkmates and counselor. Sometimes the name of your cabin—Iroquois, Comanche, Seminole—was carved on a wooden plaque and hung above the table. The table itself was either highly varnished to a sticky shine or covered with greasy oilcloth. The latter provided small amusement during boring announcements—you could flake the oiled material off its backing and onto the floor. The floor had a paradoxical surface that was perpetually sticky yet slippery at the same time, no matter how many times a day it was washed.

No doubt the stickiest seat on the dining porch was the "guest chair" at the director's table. If you were tapped to sit at the head table for some infraction of camp rules, it was an extremely uncomfortable experience. There was no one to talk to—except for the most pained conversation—and you certainly couldn't horse around. Needless to say, you had to have great manners and you had to eat all your food, too.

Service at the head table was no different than at the others: family style, with food brought to the table by waiters. Waiters were either local teenagers hired to work in the kitchen for summer jobs or campers who took care of setting the tables, waiting, and clearing. A camp director in 1929 commented on the ins and outs of being a good waiter:

Waiting on table is a highly competitive occupation. One must try to get ahead of all the other waiters, and yet do it smoothly and according to dining-room rule. One must be quickly alert, but never blunderingly precipitous. Things must come to the table hot and fast, yet the table suffers from poor and overhasty management. The group must be pleased. A poor waiter pays a price in social standing.

An important task of the table setter was making sure every table had its pair of metal pitchers full of milk and bug juice. At Camp Catawba, there were two advantages to being picked to set the table. One was finding out what was for dessert before anyone else. The other was putting the only Mickey Mouse spoon in camp at your place setting.

The assembly of the entire camp into the dining hall was often the spark that set off a round of outrageous behavior. The wise guys were wiser than ever. The loudmouths were never louder. Manners were usually at a low ebb, even though counselors were supposedly minding everyone's. Occasionally, one counselor would take his job too seriously, and if you were caught resting an elbow on the table, he'd grab you by the wrist and bang your misplaced elbow onto the table to teach "it" a lesson.

Good manners or no, mealtimes and noise went hand in hand. Some camps tried to curb this. Others accepted it with the comment, "noisy children are happy children," and as a result had a dining hall that was deafening. Songs and cheers filled any gaps in conversation and were sometimes only silenced by the bell for announcements at the end of the meal. In describing this phenomenon, one camp has gone on record as saying: "When this mess hall is filled with 180 competent diners of assorted ages one can scarcely hear himself eat. . . . Under this roof there has been boundless eating and boundless joy."

*The readied dining hall, bug juice and milk on every table, awaits the onslaught.*

### A MEAL

Boys enter, clatter, crash of chairs, soup (sometimes), meat, "Aw, gimme some bread," "Kick the cow over here." "Say, got a monopoly on the sinkers?" Bell! Speech! Clapping! Bear Lake cheer! Clatter of dishes! Waiter hurt! One butter plate gone! "Hey, waiter, use your head!" "Aw! Who ya hittin' with that tray?" "Get off my foot!" Bell! Table __ challenges Table __ to a game of __. Applause! Bell! "Boys! Boys! Please have this cheering stopped." Silence! Dessert! "Take that plate out o' your lap!" "Ain't no more?" "Say, I'm hungry. I'm gonna kick!" "All ready, let's go!" Meal over.

*Summary of a meal that appeared in* The Wigwam, *1915.*

*A picture-perfect rest hour.*

# Rest Hour

To the chagrin of most gung-ho campers, rest hour followed lunch. After the noon meal—which traditionally was the largest and heaviest of the day—all campers were obliged to trudge back to their bunks.

You could always bide some time by stopping at the canteen. It was perfectly legitimate to have to buy stamps. How else could you write home? But if you patronized the camp store too often, you were in danger of depleting your ten-dollar charge account before the summer ended. In the days of enforced haircuts, a local barber would usually visit the camp during rest hour. If your counselor announced it was time for a haircut, this was another way you could avoid your bed. But it was a trade-off, though, because no one ever really wanted to get a haircut.

By the time you reached your cabin or tent, it was time to settle in for an hour's peace and quiet. How peaceful and quiet? Well, that was another matter.

The longer the "hour," the more restless the campers became. And some camps were known to stretch rest hour to nearly *two full hours.* For part of that time, the "midget" campers, those under ten, actually slept. But once you were older than ten, rest hour became harder to take lying down.

The strict camps demanded shoes off, one to a bed, prone position, no talking. That may have occurred a few times at the beginning of the season. But the stricter the camp, the more likely you'd find kids bouncing on squeaky bedsprings, throwing pillows, and whistling and singing ("I'm not talking"). Usually campers occupied themselves with checkers, cards, jacks, Clue or Star Reporter, and low-profile merrymaking. Comic book reading was probably the most popular pastime. In 1957, a Camp Waldenite wrote this tribute:

> They've monopolized the minds of
>     everyone in camp.
> They're especially helpful when
>     the weather is kinda damp.
> They can be found on the floor of
>     every bunk,
> Under every pillow, in every trunk.
> They are the cause of our parents'
>     dirty looks.
> Yes, I'm talking about
>     Love Comic Books.

The "radical" camps permitted the campers to leave their bunks. One camper from the late twenties reminisced about

*Two means of passing the time at rest hour.*

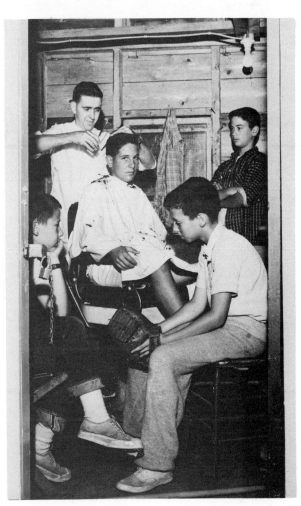

## MAIL CALL

Mail and rest hour were tied closely in the minds of campers. There was no doubt that part of rest hour was spent writing letters—it was impolite not to write to all the relatives. Some mothers packed pread-dressed and stamped postcards to the grandparents. Also, most camps required letters to parents as meal tickets at least once a week. But, being on the receiving end of mail call was what the camper was concerned about. And it was even fun to get mail before you were old enough to read, as shown in a letter to a five-year-old camper.

*Letter from parents.*

---

SUNDAY JULY 19, '42

DEAR PAL
YESTERDAY THE MAIL MAN BROUGHT US A NICE POST CARD FROM YOU IN WHICH YOU TOLD US ABOUT GOING IN SWIMMING. WE ARE VERY HAPPY BECAUSE IT IS VERY HOT HERE AND SWIMMING IS THE ONLY WAY TO KEEP COOL.

DO YOU REMEMBER THE GARDEN YOU PLANTED NEAR THE GAR-AGE? IT WAS A VICTORY GARDEN, LIKE LITTLE BROWN BEAR'S. WELL, IT IS GROWING NICELY OON WE WILL HAVE CARRIE CARROT AND BILLY BEET AND CARL CUCUM-BER AND MAYBE LATER WE SHALL HAVE TOMMY TOMATO AND LOTTIE LETTUCE TOO. WE ARE SURE THAT YOU EAT ALL THE VEGETABLES SERVED YOU IN CAMP. YOU KNOW THAT A GALLANT ALWAYS EATS HIS VEGETABLES AND SALAD. A GOOFUS POUTS AND SAYS "I DON'T LIKE VEGETABLES" OUR BOY IS A GALLANT.

GOOFUS

GALLANT

LOVE FROM GRANDMA AND AUNT DOT, AND HUGS AND KISSES FROM MOMMY & DADDY

REGARDS TO AUNT MIRIAM.

The unusual price for a bottle of Coke dates this photo to circa 1946.

## CANTEEN

It has been said that the first question 95 percent of all prospective campers asked on being interviewed was "What's the canteen like?" Although theoretically the function of the canteen was to replenish exhausted supplies of flashlight batteries, pads of paper, and film, what it really came down to was the brands of candy sold and the number of bars permitted at a single purchase. One girls' camp practiced excellent child psychology by placing a limit on the number of candy bars the younger campers could buy. But, when they were old enough to buy as many as they wanted, they started worrying about getting too fat, or pimples, and only bought one anyway. According to a camp candy survey in 1954, only 5 percent of the camps didn't allow candy at all. Perhaps those were the camps that the 5 percent of campers who didn't ask about the canteen ended up going to.

What's the schedule on a day
    that's hot?
Softball is what we've got.
Batting, running in the sun,
We all slowly tramp down after
    we're done.
Staggering campers are always seen,
Heading for the Coke machine!

Walden Splash, 1965.

*Standard reading fare in 1928.*

▼▲▼▲▼▲▼▲▼▲▼▲▼▲▼▲▼▲▼▲▼▲▼▲▼▲▼

You can't separate comic books from camp. Campers arrived clutching small libraries that were traded and added to throughout the season. One former camper recalled buying two comics each week all year and stockpiling them, unread, for summer camp. Comics in camp ranged from the "funnies"—*Little Lotta, Richie Rich,* and *Donald Duck*—to the superheroes and "love" comic books. It is safe to say that few of the *Classics Illustrated* became regular reading.

One camp in California has a comic book on permanent display (pages laminated in plastic) in their museum. When Hank Ketcham, creator of Dennis the Menace, sent his real-life son Dennis to Camp Kennolyn, he was given permission to do a comic book based on the camp. Thus, *Dennis the Menace Goes to Camp* was published in 1961 and was reprinted almost every summer for years.

▼▲▼▲▼▲▼▲▼▲▼▲▼▲▼▲▼▲▼▲▼▲▼▲▼▲▼

*Even Dennis took comics to camp.*

spending her rest hours down by the lake reading dirty books with her friends.

At least once a week rest-hour time was well spent. You had to write home, so you might as well get it over with when you were confined to quarters. It was well known that campers' letters were classics of brevity and noninformation. After all, nobody checked *what* you wrote, they just made sure you wrote. Your parents quickly got used to an entire week's adventures being summarized in three sentences.

If your counselor was lax and you could get away without writing, so much the better. But it made your mail on the receiving end a little bit unpleasant:

> Dear Pegs, Don't you *ever* write to your parents? We haven't heard from you in *10 days*—at least. There had better be a good reason for not writing, Madame, even a post card is acceptable to me, you know. Best love, Mother.

If you didn't get your mail at the camp post office after lunch, it was delivered to you at your tent or cabin during rest hour. Everyone looked forward to the camp letter carrier. (A lucky few got to sort the mail everyday.) You could almost always count on some missive from either of your parents. Your father's was typewritten, four to six lines, on business stationery . . . or maybe it was a postcard from a business trip. It was your mom who provided the real news from home—what relatives she'd seen and how the dog was doing. The once-a-summer note from Granny had a dollar enclosed "for a treat." What you really hoped for was a letter from a friend at home or at another camp that would be filled with the news you most wanted to hear.

Undoubtedly, the ultimate joy was a package from home. You didn't really know what would be in it, maybe the game you asked your mom to send or a shipment of comic books. If your birthday was in the summer, you could look forward to a slew of packages, enough to arouse the jealousies of your cabinmates. Although it was expressly forbidden to get food in the mail, most parents couldn't resist rounding out the care package with a few edibles. A salami or bag of pistachios commanded the most envy.

*Nuts, nuts,*
*That's what I'm going.*
*Nuts, nuts,*
*Everyone's knowing*
*When I get a package*
*Of pistachio nuts,*
*The scene always changes,*
*From "Oh, you're a klutz,"*
*To, "Babsie you darling,"*
*From people in ruts.*

*But the people who like me*
*Will know they'll get lots*
*Of salty-scarlet,*
*Pistachio nuts.*

Even though parents *knew* that they were breaking the camp rules by sending food, it was impossible to ignore the plaintive pleas: "Please send up some gum" (a no-no at *every* camp). "When you come up please bring a can of Hershey sirup" (it's hard to imagine sneaking that into the dining hall and getting away with it). "I still haven't gotten any packages" (a coded message asking for food of any kind).

Unless your camp went so far as to make you open all packages in front of your counselor in order to confiscate any contraband, there were ways for the determined to import food packages.

If you send packages, send food. Mark it "books" so I will know and can shoo kids from other rooms out while I open the package. Some kids have can openers so you can send cans.

The odd parent was even known to hollow out secret compartments in books to hide the forbidden fruit.

One camp director in the late 1920s lamented:

Candy is tabu at camp; save when served after meals in ration lots. But like all prohibitions of things humankind wants, the law never works perfectly. Parents agree in principle, but practice lenience. Grandmothers are worse. Herman's sent him full five pounds of those abominable pink, yellow and red candies shaped like hearts, crosses, stars, horse-shoes, etc. and stamped with "Kiss Me", "Good Boy", "You are a Flirt" and "Be My Valentine." I don't object so much to the sentiments as to the questionable inks with which they are printed, nor to the quality, as to the quantity with which I have to deal. . . . At the close of summer I shall have again, as usual, a dozen or more pounds of sweets. These I will not dare return to the boys to eat on the train. They are hardly returnable home. They will spoil before next summer. The store will not trade for watermelons or grapes. I do not like to send them to the incinerator; that is too much like a Volstead officer pouring good beer down the gutter.

There was no doubt that getting a package livened up rest hour. As the hour wore on, the unnatural silence that had been imposed upon camp began to break up as the natives got increasingly restless. Campers started to put away their books and games and put on their sneakers in anticipation of the first afternoon period. If water-skiing had been announced at lunch, some of the daredevils would always try to sneak off to the waterfront early for a good position in line. Most campers waited, though, on the steps of their tents, ready to explode forth at the first note of the bugle.

*Receiving the forbidden fruit—sourballs.*

*There's nothing left for me*
*Of what there used to be;*
*They took it all away,—*
*Yes, all my candy's gone;*
*They came to all the bunks;*
*They opened all the trunks;*
*They took it out in hunks*
*Yes, all my candy's gone.*

Somer = Settings, *volume 1, number 5, 1929.*

*Two packages in one day!*

*Budding sculptresses in smocks and sneakers, with photographic inspiration on the wall.*

# Arts and Crafts

Gimp. That plastic stuff. It came on big spools in lots of colors, with extra spools of the camp colors. Did anyone go to camp and not make a lanyard? The box stitch, the barrel stitch—the friendly arts and crafts counselors (sometimes a husband-and-wife team) could hardly wait to get those fingers weaving.

The arts-and-crafts shop usually had many separate departments. The art department began with sketching around the camp grounds and worked up to art trips to the seashore or other scenic points for watercolors or even oils. In 1924, budding Wigwam artists attacked their cardboard canvases with relish. "There were great expanses filled in an hour and a half; there was brushwork not to be exceeded in breadth and daring by Velásquez himself." At Tapawingo, in 1930, they even taught the history of art—with emphasis on the work of great animal and landscape artists, of course.

Craft projects centered around linoleum block printing, plaster casting, tooled leather and hammered copper, basketry, ceramics, carving and whittling, clay sculpture, jewelry making, and weaving. A girls' camp noted, "there are looms for all types of weaving, from the simple primitive Indian head-bands to the more intricate Indian rugs, towels and scarves." Campers were usually known more for the quantity of objects turned out, rather than the quality.

The manual arts division tackled projects as simple as a pair of bookends, a shoeshine kit, or a birdhouse, to full-size canoes and kayaks. Model-building sometimes became a mania in shop, with campers turning out rubber band–powered airplanes to compete in camp air shows. At Viking, a sailing camp on Cape Cod, boys made a different model sailboat each year they were at camp. They got progressively bigger and more complex each year and raced one another in mini-regattas.

Another arts program at camp was photography. Campers have been bringing their "Kodak cameras" along with them since the turn of the century. The photography squad was often tramping about securing pictures to be developed and printed in the camp darkroom for the camp newspaper.

Snapshots of camp pals and activities helped fill the trunk when it was time to go home, along with baskets, birch-bark lampshades, papier-mâché masks, and other treasures proudly made at camp.

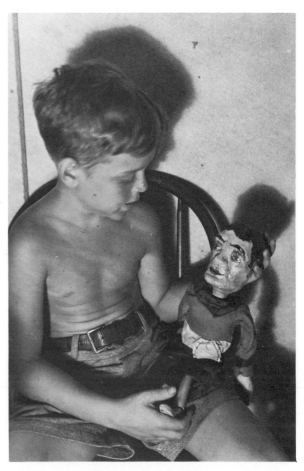

*The proud puppeteer gazes at his grotesque creation.*

Attaching the rigging to a model sailboat in preparation for the big race.

The loom room, where a single project could last the entire summer.

Who could resist making this for his dad in the ceramics shop?

At a Florida camp, rife with snakes, whittling this custom walking-stick handle was a natural.

Indian and Mexican motifs mix in the craft shop. Carved thirty years ago, these are still treasured by the proud former camper.

*Getting nowhere, fast, but learning the J-stroke.*

# Beyond Swimming

Once you passed your swimming test, a whole new world opened up to you. Aquabelles, tow ropes, oars, paddles, and jibs.

Canoes and camp were as inseparable as dragonflies and the lake. The spirit of adventure, the romance of the Indians, the tales of Lewis and Clark, the desire for a suntan infested every camper with a yearning to be out paddling and exploring the lake. Once proficient, you could go on short trips for picnics or nature hunts, or, even better, overnights away from camp.

Canoeing instruction began uncomfortably on the sandy dock with campers kneeling, paddles in the water, learning the different strokes. The basic J-stroke was mastered there, and then tried out en masse in a war canoe, with the instructors bellowing a rhythm for all campers to try to follow in unison (without scraping your paddle on the side of the canoe). Canoe safety was also mandatory—learning to avoid the rocks, how to get in and out without tipping, and how to get back in if you did fall out or tip over.

Certification of canoemanship would vary from camp to camp. To be a water-witch at Sebago-Wohelo in the teens, there were a raft of tests to pass, a number of which were basic life saving, such as undressing (down to your bathing suit, of course) in deep water without touching a boat or float. Also you had to upset—not too hard—and right—not too easy—a canoe by yourself and paddle alone on a rough day from the dock out to the war canoe and back. Only after you became a water-witch could you try sailing or aquaplaning.

For those at ease in a canoe, there were a number of games that used to be played at camp (with a slight disregard for safety). Gunwaling was always a favorite. A pair of campers would take a canoe to deep water and stand on the gunwales at either end. They would alternately bounce up and down, rocking the canoe violently, until one, the loser, fell off.

Tilting was another canoe sport with an elaborate set of rules. It involved a pair of canoes and teams of two campers. Each canoe had a paddler and a tilter. The tilter was armed with a seven-foot bamboo pole that ended in a canvas bag padded with hair stuffing. The tilter stood in the bow, usually on a seat, a platform, or the gunwales. The paddler sat in the stern and maneuvered the canoe into position near the opponent's. The point was obvious: to dislodge your opponent, knocking him to the floor of the canoe or into the water; you could also win by

*Righting a swamped canoe was tricky, but manageable, with four girls.*

*It took a lot of squaws to launch a war canoe this size. The entire camp at Sebago-Wohelo could fit in four of these craft in 1934.*

*The sail canoe at Tapawingo was a tricky combination not often found in camp.*

All styles of boats hit the water at camp: rigging the goblin at the Winona Camps (left); taking a lesson in a Sunfish at Hiawatha (above); and hiking out on Lake Winnipesaukee at Camp Kehonka (below).

*One thing rowboats were good for was an early-morning fishing expedition—one rower and two fishers from Mah-Kee-Nac try their luck.*

CANOE SONG

1 My pad-dle's keen and bright,
2 Flashing with sil-ver.
3 Fol-low the wild goose flight,
4 Dip, dip and swing.
  Dip, dip and swing her back,
  Flashing with sil-ver,
  Swift as the wild goose flies,
  Dip, dip and swing.

*Camp O-At-Ka songster.*

*Maneuvering into position and preparing for blows in a tilting match in 1917.*

disarming him. The match consisted of three rounds of ninety seconds each, with thirty-second rest periods between rounds. If no fall occurred, the winner was selected on the basis of blows struck and aggressiveness.

Less violent games included canoe races that might involve getting out of and back into your canoe at the halfway point. An interesting race was described in 1927 at Sebago-Bear Mountain Camp. Big snapping turtles were caught in nearby brooks by the boys, and holes were bored (painlessly) through the back tip of the shells. With heavy picture wire, turtles were harnessed to the bows of canoes, and races were held. Unfortunately, you couldn't steer, so the races were unpredictable. No casualties were suffered because hands and toes were kept a safe distance from the snappy beaks. One camper boasted he'd return the following summer with a bit and reins that would steer the most stubborn of the "aquarial broncos."

Some might say that rowing was the natural companion to canoeing. That may be so, but the only time you ever took a rowboat out was when all the canoes were already spoken for. Rowboats proved to be too much work for too little enjoyment —and you couldn't even see where you were going. One of the best things you could say about them was that they were nearly impossible to swamp. At least if you were canoe-shy, the rowboat could safely get you across the lake.

The most daring camper might have been the barefoot water-skier. This acrobat behind the boat had come a long way since the early days of aquaplaning. It was a relatively easy feat to be pulled around the lake on a platform. But fast boats, good instruction, and fearless campers turned the sport around, and many of the youngest campers started doing trick skiing—spinning around 360 degrees or stopping at 180 degrees and skiing backward—slaloming on difficult courses, or stepping out of their skis altogether to ski barefoot. For camps that had water-skiing (those that didn't usually cited water and noise pollution), it was often the most popular activity in camp, even for those who were slowly towed in circles on two skis around the lake, dreaming about the day they'd learn to drop one.

A sound heard frequently by the lake was the blaring music of a phonograph equipped with an extra-loud needle, playing fox trots, waltzes, and tangos, to which the synchronized swimmers did their moves: ballet legs, surface dives, skulling, and dolphins. The Aquabelles were known for their pageantry, splashless swimming, and ability to hold their breath. The girls practiced all summer long for their day of glory when they gave their show. Special costumes that could be worn in water were designed and fabricated, complete with decorated bathing caps and wristlets. Girls strained to hear the music while performing underwater stunts. (A Chinese tom-tom was occasionally used to help keep the beat.) Special problems arose when your waterfront was on a river, like it used to be at Forest Acres. Extra calculations had to be made and intensive skulling done to stay in formation while battling the current.

A quieter sport to be found on the lake was sailing. In small one- or two-man boats, campers could learn the rudiments and attempt to sail competently, after getting the basics on land. But no amount of practice on shore could prepare you for that moment of terror when the wind picked up and the boat capsized. The waterfront director, scanning the lake with binoculars from his tower, would order a rescue boat to speed out and help set things right.

The best skippers set their sails for the camp regattas, all-day events with lots of camps vying for the trophies and plaques. After traveling for one or two hours to the invitational, and being psyched for days, it was a gyp when the weather wouldn't cooperate. The director of the Winona Camps was known to bring out the foul-weather signal flag before the start of their regatta during a recent summer to try to induce the faintest breeze on an utterly calm, beautiful day. Five other camps had traveled there to take part in the races, which got off to a very slow start.

No doubt about it, there was a lot of action down on the waterfront. But until you passed that deep-water test, all you could do was hang around the paddle house, try on life jackets for size, and look on enviously.

*The water-ski instructor showed off for the girls at Tripp Lake Camp in the thirties. This was one trick that would be hard to accomplish on skis . . . and it wasn't easy on an aquaplane.*

*Attempting to touch seventy toes in a water ballet.*

*Posing above the waterfall on Trip Day at Tripp Lake Camp.*

# *Day Trips*

*The author being buried alive on an excursion to the beach.*

The most satisfying part of any day trip—before the stomach-ache set in—was treating yourself to ice-cream sodas, ice-cream sundaes, ice-cream cones, and candy—all the goodies you couldn't get enough of while you were at camp. It was also one of the few times you had some hard cash jingling around in your pocket, which you could spend at will.

Day trips were a means to get out of camp into the real world. For a few hours, you could escape briefly from the structure of first period, second period, lunch, rest hour. . . . Some camps had Trip Day once a week, when the whole place emptied out on various forays. This usually coincided with the cook's day off, so all campers were given box lunches—a bologna sandwich on white bread (without your choice of mustard or mayo), an apple, and some cookies—and sent on their way.

Trip Day for camps near the Atlantic or Pacific often meant a weekly outing to the beach. Castle building, shell collecting, body surfing, fishing off the pier, and exploring tide pools occupied campers for the entire day, punctuated frequently by a gritty hot dog, a warm soda, some gooey cotton candy, salt-water taffy, and a couple of hunks of rapidly melting white chocolate. If your camp was far from the ocean, a single beach trip a season was more like it, and the entire day was an event about which to write home:

> Dear Mom & Dad, I had a ball on our trip. On the way over we stopped at a trampoline place. When we got to Ogunquit we had lunch & took a dip. The water was 58° and some waves were taller than I am. After that we drove to Old Orchard Beach. I had a *soft* coffee ice cream cone and went on a few rides. I got a shrunken head, a rubber knife & a skeleton fingers.
>
> We ate dinner at the Cascade lodge. My meal cost $3.35. I had lobster stew, a lobster, ff's, salad & coffee ice cream for desert.

Any tourist attraction within striking distance of camp was fair game for a marauding busful of energetic campers: amusement parks or water slides, miniature golf courses or go-cart tracks. Sometimes the whole camp piled into every available vehicle for a day-long haul to the nearest ballpark for a major-league game.

Campers were wild about state or local fairs. They lasted long enough so that the whole camp could get a chance to go—

OGUNQUIT SONG
(Tune: "Show Me")

*Sunning and fun*
*We gained a ton,*
*Our hearts you've won*
*Ogunquit.*

*Fishing galore*
*Lobsters adored,*
*We want some more,*
*Ogunquit.*

*Pizza, Dairy Freeze and Cokes*
*We now are broke,*
*Thrilled by our yokes.*

*Dramatics, antics free*
*Our shopping sprees,*
*All was superb.*

*Now we are home*
*Fun we've been shown,*
*Thanks Mrs. Cohen.*
*Ogunquit, Ogunquit!*

*Walden Splash, 1958.*

85

*Campers on a trip passing by this famous signpost in Maine would have to stop for the obligatory group portrait.*

WE'RE OFF ON A TRIP
*(Tune: "When Johnny Comes Marching Home Again")*

*We're off on a trip, we're going away
Today, today
We've packed our sacks, and have our snacks,
We're on our way
With a cheerful heart and a carefree song
We'll be back before too long
So good-bye campers
Trippers now are we.*

Camp Tapawingo songbook.

86

without everyone going at once, which really would have been a counselor's nightmare. In 1928, a group of Somerset girls, "deciding to make the most of a fair day went to one." They were each given one dollar for spending money, nearly all of which was spent on merry-go-round rides and other "merry rounds," so that orangeade was all they could afford for supper. They all met at the sideshow to see the strong man before leaving.

He called for as many people as wanted to come and sit on a beam, to be raised in mid-air, which he was to lift. We Somerset girls, as obliging as ever, offered our lives, or rather our weight to him. All that need be said is that he lifted the beam. Of our white faces, quaking bodies, and of the partially hidden jack, I make no mention.

And then there were the educational outings. Camps organized trips to nearby summer music festivals or dance festivals, with varying degrees of camper enthusiasm and participation. (It sounded good to parents in the camp brochures, though.) If your camp was located near a summer-stock theater you got to see a *real* play to augment the camp repertoire.

There were any number of nature-related trips and hikes to build up the nature museum's collections. One favored by Wigwam in the thirties and forties was a specimen-gathering journey to the tourmaline quarries forty miles from camp. The 1940 trip was written up in their nature magazine. The hardest part of the trip was the climb up to the quarry at the top of Green Mountain, along a road described as "made of two deep ruts filled with water with slippery mud in between." When the summit was gained, and after box lunches were devoured, the boys set about madly hunting for tourmaline, a semiprecious stone. There was "sometimes a little squabbling over the choice spots for digging." Many campers procured "valuable" pieces, which were appraised by a worker at the quarry. Some were worth as much as fifty cents. "After about an hour of hunting, we climbed or slipped down the mountain, our pockets filled with stones, our faces covered with mud, and our legs covered with scratches."

There were always short mountain climbs and day hikes to be made. Those undaunted Somerset girls of 1930 were an ambitious lot. They would think nothing of hiking more than seven miles from camp to Waterville, to be "able to parade from one five-and-ten-cent store to another." Luncheon in the

On Trip Day, "soon after breakfast everyone has gone from camp—by truck, motorboat, canoes, sailboats, rowboats or on foot." (Above) *Girls take the cog railway up Mt. Washington. (Below) Suitably equipped campers gathered at the flagpole for a hike.*

*Campers are camouflaged among the rocks during a trip to the quarry.*

HIKE ALONG
*(Tune: "Caisson Song")*

*Hike along, hike along!*
*Cheer the way with lusty song.*
*For we all love the red and the blue.*
*Shake a leg, shake a leg*
*'Cause it's not a wooden peg.*
*Somerset always forges ahead.*
*With a heigh-heigh-o*
*And a cheerio we go*
*Somerset is the best camp we know.*
*Keep in step, keep in step,*
*March along with loads of pep,*
*Somerset, we are rooting for you,*
*Keep a'rooting*
*Somerset, we are rooting for you.*

*Camp Somerset songster.*

Chinese restaurant preceded the buying sprees, and refreshments at Spear's ice-cream parlor followed. Few girls, however, wanted to hike all the way back to camp on full stomachs and carrying packages. Luckily there was a trolley that went half way back. One of the girls wrote, "During the ride we learned to appreciate our training in horse-back riding, for we felt very much at home being bumped around constantly."

Though many hikes passed through town, and frequently right by a soda fountain, most didn't have it as their *final* objective. The *Camp Abnaki Handbook* of 1921 described five hikes, ranging in length from six to sixteen miles. The shortest was to W. B. Dodds's stock farm, where the campers could view "a large farm with a fine herd of Holstein cattle"—what every camper surely wanted to see.

Another hike, of twelve miles, was to the Carrying Place, a narrow part of the island on which the camp was located. This neck, only a hundred feet wide, was a place across which boats could be quickly carried. The handbook noted, "It was extensively used by smugglers from 1805 to 1810, and old lead bullets and pieces of Indian pottery are often found." The thought of actually finding some of this booty was enough to convince most to make the hike.

Any camp located near foothills or small mountains constantly sent off groups of willing campers to scale the heights by well-beaten paths. Often the youngest camper had the most energy. In the thirties it was "Flippy" at Camp Samoset: "He's only six but he won't ever let anybody get ahead of him."

At Camp Catawba every Wednesday was Hike Day, and there was no getting out of it. The rules were strict: no complaining of thirst, hunger, or exhaustion; no asking "How much farther?"; and no campers ahead of the lead counselor or behind the last one.

No matter how mundane the hike or how many times you hiked it, there could always be a twist. On a Camp Samoset journey the following story was reported in 1939:

One day when we went up to the Cascades Don caught a little red lizard and put it in his canteen. On the way home we stopped to play baseball in a field and Don hid his canteen in the bushes. Jackie got thirsty and he found it and took a big drink. And he swallowed the lizard! But it digested all right. The doctor said it would. But I guess it scratched his throat quite a lot.

✸ ✸ ✸ ✸ ✸ ✸ ✸ ✸ ✸ ✸ ✸ ✸ ✸ ✸ ✸ ✸

### No Hike Complete Without One
#### by Billy Fisher

We've all seen this fellow on the hike—it is impossible to imagine a hike without one of his type.

In the morning he comes prepared for the march arrayed in khaki hiking pants, khaki blouse, puttees, equipped with hunter's knife, camper's compass, canteen, mess kit, and all the other paraphernalia of an amateur hiker. For the first half-hour of the journey, he continually calls out in that jubilant tone of voice peculiar to his type, "Is everybody happy?" For the first ten of fifteen times this occurs, his companions answer "Yes," in the same jubilant tone, but as the road becomes hotter and dustier, and the tempers of the campers become shorter, he is told to keep his mouth shut, in no uncertain terms and tones.

The first sign of his weakening comes when after an hour or so of hiking, he begins to ask continually how far they are from their destination, and when they are going to stop for a rest. When he is informed that the hike has only begun, he begins to lag behind, and one of his companions is compelled to carry his knapsack for him in order not to delay their progress. Finally, when he complains more and more of the blisters on his feet and the weight of his equipment, his friends are forced to hail a car and have him sent home. Truly a great hiker!

✸ ✸ ✸ ✸ ✸ ✸ ✸ ✸ ✸ ✸ ✸ ✸ ✸ ✸ ✸ ✸

*From the Greylock* Beacon, *July 15, 1931.*

*Boys enjoying the well-earned view atop Bear Mountain.*

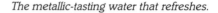

*The metallic-tasting water that refreshes.*

*Curious wayside attractions brought camp vehicles to a screeching halt.*

*All eyes are glued to the boiling water contest, a standard campcraft drill, clearly being won by the camper on the right.*

# Campcraft

No girl is considered a sport who camps out with so luxurious a thing as a pillow. Oh, no, a sweater is greatly preferable,—yet it has its drawbacks. Every camp sweater has six buttons, yet there is no way that that sweater can be rolled, pounded, turned, folded, punched or pulled, but that all six buttons penetrate the unfortunate head of the owner. My advice to future outdoor campers is, that they remove all buttons from their sweaters before nightfall.

Such were the astute observations of a Walden camper following a mostly sleepless night in 1916. Camping out, whether on camp grounds or at a remote outpost, was always part of the summer activities. In the earliest days, when you went off to summer camp, you went *camping*. Eventually, tents and cabins sprung up, but at first it was sleeping in the open *and* cooking your own meals that made the camp experience.

Camping out challenged the ingenuity of even the most fervent would-be woodsman. When the tent leaked in the middle of the night for no apparent reason the problem had to be solved. The troublesome twig poking the canvas had to be located and removed. When all dry kindling got soaked during the night, and not a dry stick was to be found anywhere, you learned to store a supply under cover for such emergencies. You discovered matches would have kept better in a corked bottle than in a pocket on a rainy night, and if they'd been near a ticking watch, you could have found them easily when you frantically groped for them in the dark.

Among the first campcraft skills to learn was building a shelter and making your own bed and sleeping in it. At Camp Unalayee, campers teamed up in pairs and, using no tools, had two hours to build a shelter out of sticks, branches, leaves, and dirt. That night they tried them out, without sleeping bags, only their clothes. The next day, the truth came out. Some had to be awakened at dawn, they slept so well and were so toasty. Others were up at 4:00 A.M., after tossing, turning, and shivering all night long, finally trying to get warm next to a fire.

Anyone who wanted to camp out had to learn to make a campfire. The standard exercise to gauge your skill was the boiling water test: A camper had five minutes to make a fire and bring a cup of water to boil, using only one match—and *no* paper. Materials were already at hand, but the trick, after getting the fire started, was to have enough pieces of *dry* wood of the right sizes to keep the fire burning hot.

*To concoct a "spit in the eye" one puts a pat of butter in the pan, makes a hole in the center of a piece of bread, and fries an egg therein.*

*Advanced campers pose between their just-built lean-to and reflector oven.*

91

*A pensive Kennebec camper keeps a watchful eye on his weenie.*

Tune from *H.M.S. Pinafore*

*Give three cheers for the J.M.G.'s*
*Who clear the brush and chop the trees,*
*Who make the fires*
*And cook the meals*
*And clean up all the potato peels.*
*They do their work with the greatest of ease,*
*Though smoke sometimes makes them cough and*
    *sneeze,*
*They bake the cake and cook the stew,*
*Do all the things they ought to do.*
*As the gay voices sing*
*And the ax blades ring,*
*In the beech and pine you'll see us dine.*
*We'll rise at dawn, get up and yawn,*
*And go back to work again.*
*So give three cheers for the J.M.G.'s*
*Who clear the brush and chop the trees.*
*We've done our best and are proud to claim*
*A permanent place in the State of Maine.*
                    — *Camp Bendito*

*An ode to the Junior Maine Guides.*

Once you mastered the art of fire-building (not too big, not too hot), the world of outdoor cooking opened up. Although it might have been just weenies and marshmallows speared on green sticks, it was by no means limited to that. Even the youngest campers could learn to rustle up some griddlecakes. At Camp Matoaka in the 1920s, the girls fashioned individual cook stoves out of number 10 cans. The cans were upturned and the bottom was used for a pan. A four-inch-square hole was cut in the side to feed the fire, and a smaller hole on the other side near the top created a draft. The girls could feast on French toast, bacon and eggs, corn fritters, fried tomatoes, or of course, pancakes. As one said, "You could cook, eat, and keep the fire going at the same time."

But this fare was rudimentary compared to some. Boys at O-At-Ka enjoyed chocolate cake made from scratch and baked in a reflector oven, while girls at Sebago-Wohelo ground their own wheat and then made and baked bread by the open fire.

The Junior Maine Guide program, offered at many camps, turned out expert cooks. One of the tests a JMG had to pass to earn his certificate required him to cook a full meal, that is, a roast; chowder or stew; a bread, biscuits, or cornbread; and a cake. Not only that, it definitely had to taste good. "The Junior Guide must offer his dishes to the discriminating palate of men long experienced in woods cookery."

It usually took two summers' worth of preparation to pass the JMG battery of tests given during a three-day period in the wilds of remote northern Maine. Expertise was required in subjects ranging from axemanship to first aid, natural history to no-trace camping. This was the last word in campcraft, and many a JMG from years gone by is still mighty proud of his patch earned in the woods.

For the average camper, a program like the Junior Guides' was way beyond the call of duty. Most campers were interested in campcraft just for use in overnight hiking and canoe trips. The fun of camping out and cooking such delights as hobo stew—hamburger, sliced potatoes and carrots wrapped in tin foil and thrown on the coals—and s'mores—that quintessential camp dessert made of graham crackers, toasted marshmallow, and four squares of a Hershey chocolate bar—made it all worthwhile. With a hearty meal under their belts, it was time to make up the beds—pine boughs and blankets for the hearty, and down sleeping bags on Ensolite pads for the rest—and turn in.

When these last few items have been settled, the moon rises upon the supposed-to-be slumberers. Every individual thinks that she is the only one wide awake and uncomfortable, and lies perfectly still, so that no one should notice this fact.

92

*At Camp Unalayee (above and below) every meal is a cookout and a cleanup by campers and counselors.*

*Some campers pride themselves on never having spent a night in the infirmary during their camp career; but for most it was hard to avoid at least one trip there.*

# To Your Health

The least-used building in camp, most years, was the infirmary. It wasn't a place where anyone wanted to go, unless you happened to be in love with the camp nurse (and there was always someone every year who was). Or, as a last resort, it was sometimes used to duck out of an unpopular activity.

Mostly the infirmary was the place where minor cuts and scrapes were daubed with iodine and bandaged and where calamine lotion was liberally dispensed to poison ivy sufferers. It was also the storehouse for "more allergy medicine than the biggest hospital in New York City." However, when it came to serious illness, the infirmary was superseded by the local hospital. No matter where a camp was located, it always boasted of being within minutes of a modern, well-equipped hospital.

Contagious diseases were the bane of all camps. Not only did they make for an unpleasant summer, but your camp might end up being quarantined by other camps, eliminating sports and social events. In 1917, at Kennebec, a special "internment camp" was set up by the doctor due to an outbreak of impetigo. The log for the season described weeding "the Imps from the Angels and place [ing] them in purgatory." It was known as Imp Village. One healthy camper charged other campers a pack of gum for a secret tour of "the strange creatures in Ringworm Village." The Imps cooperated by performing native dances, and the guide lectured on the subject. The best part of the epidemic was that the camp installed hot showers thereafter.

During the forties and early fifties, polio was a very real threat at every camp. Because no one knew how it was contracted, no one knew how to prevent it. During the polio scares, every possible precaution was taken, including barring visitors to camp, discontinuing trips to town, and having counselors who'd been out of camp wash and gargle before rejoining the camp. The sudden disappearance of a camper sent home sparked fear among campers, who lived from rumor to rumor. In fact, camp was safer than the cities, and it was not uncommon for the season to be extended to avoid returning to infected areas.

But epidemics struck rarely. Usually the nurse was more preoccupied with mundane matters such as fat kids' diets and thin kids' extra meals. Many camps had "skinny lunches," where eggnogs, milk shakes, and malteds were dispensed between meals to those underweight. Everyone had to submit to a regular weigh-in, which no doubt caused consternation at the girls' camps. There was no way of escaping visits to the infirmary.

PERFECT POSTURE (Round)
(Tune: "Frère Jacques")

*Perfect posture, perfect posture,*
*Do not slump, do not slump,*
*You must grow up handsome,*
*You must grow up handsome,*
*Hide that hump, hide that hump.*

*Part of the health program at many girls' camps included posture classes. At Camp Fernwood, good posture armbands were distributed weekly to deserving campers. At Alford Lake Camp, they even wrote a song about it.*

*Two resident nurses waiting for business on a slow day.*

*One of the favorite evening programs at any camp was theater night. Some camps staged seven full productions in eight weeks.*

# Behind the Footlights

Many stars of stage and screen (without mentioning names) made their debuts on the boards of an outdoor theater at camp. The music, theater, and dance programs always provided what was for some a welcome alternative to the athletic field, as well as a lot of entertainment in the evenings.

Cabin skits forced everyone to get involved in theatrics. One performance from every cabin group was required for presentation to the whole camp. Shy campers competed with vigor for bit parts with no speaking involved, whereas the hams vied for the leading roles. If it was your first exposure to being behind the footlights, it either scared you permanently off the stage or left you hungering for better roles and more applause.

A far cry from the lowly cabin skit was the full-length camp production, with story, sets, and costumes varying from elaborate to corny. A catalog from Camp Tapawingo in the 1940s stated, "Shakespearian dramas, plays of Rostand, Barrie, Anatole France, and of other famous writers have been produced." But usually the fare was more down to earth.

There were always camp standards and camp favorites. In the teens it was minstrel shows, as described in a Greylock rhyme:

*Swashbucklers in sneakers mark this as a camp production. Camp costumes were usually improvised from materials at hand, and white socks and madras watchbands could be overlooked.*

> *1916*
> *Inauguration: Minstrel Show;*
> *We start in small; but watch us grow!*
> *1917*
> *Second season on the stage,*
> *Minstrelcy is still the rage.*

Gilbert and Sullivan were long-time camp specialties, especially at boys' camps. With no girls around, the lads were usually most willing to dress and assume the female parts. These full-blown presentations occupied as many as fifty singing campers and counselors. The Greylock history of camp drama in rhyme chronicled three consecutive years of successful Gilbert and Sullivan productions:

> *1936*
> *G. and S. get in their licks,*
> *"Iolanthe" really clicks.*
> *1937*
> *Hail! Brittania rules the waves!*
> *"Pinafore" earns critics' "raves."*
> *1938*
> *"Mikado" does the dipsy-do*
> *in Greylock's "Town of Lilipu."*

A sampling of the 1928 repertoire of the Walden bunks.

Four boys on the boards in Gilbert and Sullivan's H.M.S. Pinafore.

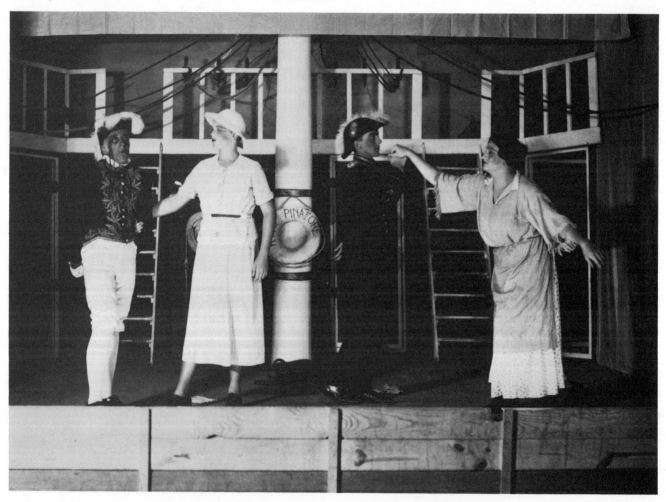

When the National Music Camp gathered its campers, a show was staged that was hard to beat. Here was the celebration for its twenty-fifth season.

Girls in formation present a tableau by the lake.

*A percussion band in rehearsal in the lodge.*

*An ensemble of wind instruments practiced on stumps, except for the bassoonist, who was too short to sit down.*

Theater at camp was so varied that anyone who wanted to take part could find a niche. It was so much fun that almost everyone in camp got involved. Although the starring roles *usually* went to those with the most talent, there was always room for one more in a mob scene or a chorus. Similarly, in stagecraft, even the least artistic could find happiness in slopping a coat of paint onto a one-color flat.

All summer long, show tunes from camp musicals were whistled and hummed, especially after rehearsals, but even on the bus to a baseball game or in the lodge before dinner. Music was part of daily life at camp . . . from reveille to taps. Grace in the dining hall was often sung, and mealtime itself was filled with singing. Visitors to camp were often singled out with welcoming songs, sung by the entire camp, but orchestrated by song leaders. It wasn't unusual for a table of campers to burst into song unprovoked at any time during the meal, and the effect was contagious. With all this extemporaneous vocalizing going on throughout the meal, it was a wonder how anybody got in a mouthful.

Campers were well known for their uncanny ability to borrow a melody and coin a ditty on *any* subject or personality in camp. The best of the impromptu songs became part of the camp repertoire, with the authors getting up in front of the whole gang to teach the lyrics, like this one from Camp Tapawingo:

THE DAY'S COME ROUND
*Tune: "Hi Ho"*

*The day's come round, to look thru lost*
    *and found.*
*I've lost my blues, my saddle shoes and*
    *I've looked all around.*
*I cannot find those clothes I've left*
    *behind, I've searched*
*And searched all over Tap,*
*Where is that bathing cap? I think*
*I spy my regulation tie, my mother*
    *sewed the name tapes on,*
*She'd die if they were gone.*
*And finally there's nothing left for me,*
*I have once more, what I had before,*
*Now ends my plea.*

If your parents made you bring your instrument to camp, practice and instruction had to be worked into your schedule. Many camp bands were formed, beginning with the lowly harmonica, and this actually made your instrument and talent desirable, instead of a liability. At Pemigewassett, prospective campers were asked, "Do you want to play on the banjo or ukulele or cornet or saxophone or drum or trombone? Would you care to be in an orchestra or band and assist in giving concerts in the villages or girls' camps?" What an enticement! A trip to a girls' camp, followed by a dance, has been known to swell the ranks of many camp bands.

The band at Pemi traditionally gave five or six concerts a year, some on village greens, where townspeople would listen from their cars and honk their approval. In order to make up a full band, staff members were sometimes hired because of an ability to play the tuba or trumpet. For many years a camper marched along with an oboe and no reed, because it *looked* so impressive to have an oboe in the band.

But all this was amateur compared to what has been going on since 1928 at the National Music Camp at Interlochen. Here campers brought their instruments because they wanted to, and took part in some of the hundreds of concerts, recitals, drama, and dance productions that took place during the eight-week season. Intensive training in one of the arts was combined with sports, recreation, and other traditional camp activities. It should be noted, though, that an article about the National Music Camp from 1935 mentioned that baseball was not offered, "because of the real danger which ofttimes occurs to musicians from 'baseball finger.' "

The art of dance was taught mainly at girls' and coed camps. In the 1934 *Handbook of Summer Camps,* Porter Sargent wrote not quite convincingly:

Dancing is a normal activity for virile, bearded, muscular men. There's nothing effeminate about it. Think of the war dance of the American Indians and Zulus, of the snake dance of our young collegians after the football games. Among the primitive tribes dancing is largely the pre-rogative of the male.

However, with the exception of square, folk, and a little Indian dancing, not much dance was taught to boys at camp, and for this they were thankful. For girls it was another story. As a camper wrote in 1928, "I cannot see how a camper, blessed by the freedom of camp uniform, and surrounded by such constant beauty and joy, can keep from dancing spontaneously and joy-ously at least once a day."

During certain periods in camp history, dance has reigned supreme at girls' camps. In 1935, Camp Chattooga in Georgia built its whole program around it, and as a result had girls in diaphanous costumes dancing all day long around camp. These so-called nature dances were done out-of-doors, using the trees, the lake, and the sunset as props. The setting-up exercises were replaced by a ceremonial dance to the sun, and, in the evening, another dance around the campfire sent the girls to bed with pleasant dreams and stretched, tired muscles.

Throughout the thirties, classic dance had campers dressed in cheesecloth or swimsuits flitting continually about the camp or presenting tableaux with the lake as a backdrop. More re-cently this mania gave way to ballet and gymnastics, with the amusing images of the young nymphs of yesteryear relegated to former campers' scrapbooks.

*Girls in leopard skin costumes dance an Egyptian number in a natural forest setting.*

*Striking a modern dance pose on the way to the waterfront.*

*A group of campers gets a small send-off from cabinmates. The crowds will be bigger to hear the stories of the adventures on their return.*

# Overnights

When you think of long trips away from camp, you think of portaging heavy canoes over short distances that seemed interminable, sore muscles from endless paddling, and spending the night squished beneath your overturned canoe in order to keep the rain from soaking you. Or you recall blister upon blister inside new hiking boots, slapping at gnats and black flies, and more aching muscles from a perpetual uphill climb.

On the other hand, the rewards made it all worthwhile: successfully running the rapids without swamping your canoe; the serenity of floating down a river with only your friends around; the incredible views from mountain peaks; skinny-dipping in spring-fed lakes and brooks.

For most campers, an extended canoe trip of three to five days was long enough . . . unless it was the tradition of the camp to gradually work up, year by year, to marathon trips. Whatever the length, the basic pattern was the same: up before dawn on departure day to load your duffel (packed the night before); off to the trip shack to pick up the wannigans—canoe storage boxes loaded with food and cooking utensils; then after a hasty breakfast, piling into the camp truck and heading for your embarkation point with canoe trailer rattling behind.

The next few days were filled with paddling and portaging, eating and sleeping, setting up and breaking camp. The natural diversion on any canoe trip was fishing. A camper's log from a North Woods trip commented on the boys' luck: "We launched the canoes and went fishing. Everybody nearly caught around five fish but nobody quite succeeded in catching anything." In the meantime, the counselor on shore whipping up the "Aunt Jemimas" was so nervous that the campers would hook one another with their wild and frenzied casting "that he put too much water in the pancakes and they would not be made bigger than a silver dollar."

However, other canoeists have been known to subsist quite luxuriously on fish caught while afloat. On an extended trip, the boys from Camp Manito-wish in Wisconsin succeeded in bringing home twenty-four bass in less than an hour, and threw back as many more. Boys from Camp Kittatinny, fishing virgin waters in Canada, racked up two hundred and twelve fish in fourteen days and brought back to camp "many cleaned and prepared fish heads of the great northern pike and the heavy fighting lake trout. These heads have been attractively mounted on appropriate plaque boards since."

*Backpacking meant more than just hoisting a pack in 1919 —girls carried many things by hand as well, including water buckets, cooking pots, and hatchets.*

CANOE TRIP SONG
(Tune: "We're in the Money")

*We're back from Somerset,*
*And our trip was the best,*
*We did a lot of things and boy,*
  *did we have fun!*

*Just back from Somerset,*
*And we're all full of zest,*
*We've just returned, but we all*
  *wish we'd just begun.*

*We did a lot of paddling,*
  *and cooking, and such,*
*And we're all here to tell you*
  *that our cooking sure did beat*
  *the Dutch.*

*We're back from Somerset,*
*And, girls, this is the test,*
*You've got to rough it, tough it,*
  *and we've got the stuff.*
*Camp Somerset, 1933.*

Tune: "List to Me While I Tell You"

*Listen well, while we tell you*
*Of a trip that was mapped out for us,*
*Listen well while we tell you*
*Of our marvelous trip, it was thus,*
*We went to a camp called Tohoma,*
*We never saw girls so polite,*
*They took us in swimming, canoeing and dancing,*
*And asked us to stay over-night.*
*We did*
*You bet.*
*Next day we went off on our trip,*
*We climbed Moosalaki and then through Lost River*
  *we squoze,*
*We spent heaps of money,*
*And sleeping in tents we all froze.*
*Next morning we started again*
*Saw Agassiz Basin, and then*
*O! the Flume, it was great,*
*The Old Man of the Mountain was also first rate,*
*Who could kick*
*It was slick!*
*And much to our liking*
*Although 'twas called hiking*
*We rode through New Hampshire all day.*

*Walden Camp Songs, 1926.*

104

Campers looked forward to every meal. You got so hungry being outdoors twenty-four hours a day and working so hard. The food cooked on the campfire just tasted that much better. And also, whether it was stated or implied, there was always a competition to turn out a feast that would top the last one. Campers and counselors rustled up such delights as: "soup, stew, cocoa and pineapple upside-down-cake" or "beef steak, fried potatoes and onions, blueberry pie (fresh-picked by the gang) and cocoa."

The least likeable aspect of any canoe trip had to be the portages—those stretches on land between lakes and rivers where you carried your canoes and gear. Short carries were usually accomplished with a minimum of unpleasantness, but they weren't always short, as recorded in one camper's story of a trip to Canada. After struggling up the side of a steep hill, where three steps up were followed by two slipped back, the crest was reached. It was "mule footing" on the way down as well, through dense underbrush and over fallen trees.

The final hundred yards before the new lake was reached was achieved only after struggling through the hip-high oozing muck which stuck to one's legs like fresh taffy before pulling. I recall vividly one of the fellows plugging through the mud morass and finally getting just about to the edge of the lake with the canoe when, to his disgust and the amusement of his fellow canoe trippers, he sank into the muck bath, up to his neck.

One legendary route over one hundred fifty miles in the north woods of Maine was described by a Kennebec counselor —who led generations of boys down its waterways—as "the best canoe trip in the world." The Allagash River trip has been traveled every year by Kennebec since 1909. Known as a long, hard trip that turned boys into men, all Kennebec campers worked toward passing the rigorous water and canoe tests in preparation for the Allagash trip they would make during their last season in camp.

At one of the launching areas, a warning sign was posted by the state of Maine:

For the next few miles this river can be extremely dangerous and you may become injured or lose your life. This section of the river should not be navigated except by properly equipped, qualified and experienced persons. You are urged to choose another point of entry such

*A well-documented early canoe trip under the watchful eye of the male counselor (suitably dressed in a necktie). The photos show essentials of a good trip: hard work, a great outdoor meal, and well-earned rest.*

A ragtag lot is ready to head back to camp after several days on the river.

MARCHING ALONG
(Tune: "Caissons Go Rolling Along")

Rise, boys, arise, come and join
    our merry throng
As we go swinging and marching
    along;
Our hearts light and gay as we sing
    along the way
Of Camp Greylock, the Red and the
    Grey.
Yo-ho! for the road, the sandy
    dusty road
Is calling us merrily onward.
So come with your pack upon your
    sturdy back
For Camp Greylock is marching along.

Camp Greylock songster.

as Carry Brook. No emergency system exists to assist you if you should be injured.

Although the traditional Allagash trip held special meaning for Kennebec campers, it was also traveled by many other camps. A group of boys from Androscoggin, in Maine, wrote the story of their nine-day trip in the 1937 yearbook. En route to the river, many lakes and fields had to be traversed. At one point a stiff wind broke out, and ponchos were tied to paddles to make the most of the breeze. One camper, "a poncho corner tied to one ankle, another tied to a gunwale, one arm holding a third, the last under him, looked like an octopus trying to roll himself up in a blanket."

Upon reaching the Allagash, the fun began. The first rapids proved too swift for the boys, and all canoes were roped together. The campers waded alongside, slipping on rocks, stubbing toes, and barking shins. "Shortly after noon we started again, leaving several beautiful gobs of gray paint on enterprising rocks, some of which had been previously daubed up by Kennebec."

Thereafter followed five more days of running—or walking—the rapids, interspersed with peaceful stretches, memorable overnight stays, leaking canoes, patching the same, and a fair amount of bailing.

Shortly before the end of the trip, the only big town on the river was reached. Here the campers raided all three stores for available supplies of candy, ice cream, peanuts, and crackers. These would hold them for one more day until the camp truck picked them up at their destination, Fort Kent. Naturally, the long ride back to camp was punctuated by frequent stops for hamburgers and soda at roadside diners.

Big hiking trips often started out in the same manner as canoe trips: You were driven to the starting point and were picked up afterward. This was not always the case, however. In the early days of camping, hikes started on foot from camp, no matter what the distance. The girls from the Highland Nature Camp on Sebago Lake in Maine used to hike the sixty-one miles to Mt. Washington in New Hampshire, in order to climb the peak, and then would hike the sixty-one miles back.

Similarly, boys from Camp Wigwam made a fifty-eight-mile trek each way in order to scale Mt. Washington, and they left a detailed record of the 1913 sojourn in the camp magazine. A

provision wagon pulled by horses accompanied the thirteen hikers. After the first night on the road, they democratically decided to quicken their pace, and shorten the trip from twelve to ten days. Lodging—permission to set up camp in a cow pasture or donkey field—was negotiated with farmers along the route each night.

As this was the first extended trip in Wigwam's history, the camp was telephoned at every opportunity. Each drugstore passed was visited for ice cream, candy, and "postals bought for the enlightenment of fond parents whose darlings were raising the dust on Maine and New Hampshire highways."

The food carried with the boys did not always fare too well in the August heat. "They said microbes and carbon dioxide were responsible, but suffice it to say that the beans *needed* catsup in generous quantities." Milk, at least, was fresh, as it was bought right from farmers on a daily basis.

The trudge was generally uneventful, with not much to look at save "two solid walls of forest enclosing the road." Then the rains came, and the boys headed for the mansion of a local Civil War veteran. The old goat invited them in and regaled them with stories of his wartime days, before finally offering the required night's shelter.

When the base of Mt. Washington was finally reached, the parents and sisters of one of the campers, who were vacationing nearby, arrived in an auto and invited the whole group to have dinner with them at a nearby hotel. "An almost hysterical delight at the happy turn of events ensued."

The day of the great assault on the mountain itself began at 5:15 A.M. After a half-hour search, the trail was found and the boys hiked upward. Six miles later they reached a view "the equal of which few of the fellows had ever seen." From there, the distant peak of Mt. Washington, their goal, was plainly seen. After five and a half hours of climbing they reached the summit with a great feeling of accomplishment, having made it to the top of the highest mountain east of the Rockies. Their only disappointment was that they hadn't taken the same path a local girls' camp had used to ascend at practically the same hour.

The Presidential Range—of which Mt. Washington is a part —remains a favorite hiking area for many camps in the Northeast. Camp Tapawingo's recent jaunts through the Mt. Washington area have been far cries from the rough, unpredictable trip the Wigwammers took in the teens. The emphasis was no longer

*Backpacking in California's Trinity Alps in the 1960s—
pegged pants and tennis shoes were a small improvement
over baggy bloomers and stockings that snagged on the
underbrush.*

only on getting to the peaks and conquering them; it was also
on experiencing everything the mountains had to offer a hiker.

In the Tapawingo description of a range trip, girls were
primed for what to expect. During their week-long trip, three
ranges of the White Mountains were to be traversed. They would
have the chance to hike over arctic tundra regions, formed by
the last glaciers, rarely seen south of the Yukon. Here plants
grew to less than an inch high, and few types of animals could
survive. From the tundra, it would only be one day's journey to
virgin spruce forests, so thick that the sun could not reach the
floor. After more hiking, the girls could look forward to one of
the most bizarre natural environments: Mt. Jackson's quaking
bog. If there had been enough rain, the weight of the hikers
would cause the ground to move up and down beneath them.
By the end of the week, the girls would have worked their way
across four of the highest peaks in the Northeast. This rugged
trip, limited to six seniors, was described by the head of the trip
department as "certainly safer than trying to get across the street
in New York City."

All experiential wonderment aside, any long trip still remained a contest between yourself and the elements—one you
didn't always win. At the same time, you attempted to maintain
a subsistence level of comfort. A boy from Camp Waldron in the
1940s recalled what for him turned out to be a fiasco of a hike.
Not only did he and his mates have to go through areas infested
by deer flies, but the dried fruit he was eating all along the way
gave him diarrhea, which constantly sent him into the woods.
Meanwhile, all campers were apportioned food to carry, and it
was his lot to take the jars of maple syrup, which he wrapped in
his blankets. After supper he discovered the jars had broken and
his bedding was soaked through. With no place to sleep, and
still running into the woods for relief—where he was eaten alive
by mosquitoes—he gave up trying to have a good time, forgot
about sleeping, and waited for dawn.

Most trips were still a success despite small calamities such
as bugs, bad weather, broken backpacks, and damaged canoes.
As the director of Camp Dudley in New York State jokingly remarked at a camp reunion: "Last summer we sent out one
hundred and ten trips. One hundred and nine came back. You
*know* that's a good average."

If you brought the fishing counselors along with you, you were assured of a good catch on your trip.

HIKING SONG
(Tune: "Coming thru the Rye")

If a blister meet a blister
    On a Walden toe,
Start in singing hiking song
    And watch the blisters go.

*Walden Camp Songs, 1926.*

An adventuresome group of ten marchers for an overnight. Presumably the provisions are following in a truck.

*With "free" space covered, the bingo game starts on a rainy afternoon.*

# Rainy Day

*Rain, rain, rain, just buckets of rain.*
*Pools, rivers, lakes in everybodies tent.*

As I woke the first things I noticed were the jumble of beds in the middle of my tent and the shelf covered over with raincoats. One of my tentmates slept the whole night with an umbrella over her head.

There was nothing worse than a rainy day at camp. Bad weather precipitated an abrupt change in the daily routine (not usually for the better), often beginning at wake-up. If it was raining cats and dogs, you were allowed to sleep for an extra half hour, as there wasn't much to get up for. At Camp Catawba, where traditionally you were awakened with music, the campers quickly came to recognize Handel's *Water Music* as an indicator of rainy-day activities.

In some respects, lying on your cot and listening to the patter of the rainfall on the canvas tent was a pleasant way to start the day, but rain certainly made it harder than usual to get up. For the trip down to breakfast, yellow slickers and olive ponchos were the rule, along with rubbers over sneakers, or rainboots. If it only rained one day, you could stay fairly dry walking through the woods, beneath the shelter of the immense pines. But after several days of soaking rain, the trees began to drip, and even after the storm subsided, it continued to "rain" in the woods.

Some things didn't change, even in the rain. You could still go to riflery if the range was covered. The craft shops were overcrowded. There was always fencing on the stage of the theater or the porch of the lodge. (The theater might well be occupied with rehearsals for upcoming productions.)

A rainy day was always a good day for the camp newspaper office. Those who didn't usually have the time to work on it spent part of the day typing articles, drawing cartoons, and making up puzzles for the publication.

A giant bingo game in the lodge was the focus of the day, with game prizes of giant-size suckers and candy bars. Other standard rainy-day procedures included piling into a school bus to head into town to spend an hour or so at a bowling alley or roller-skating rink.

No doubt some campers looked forward to rainy days—as long as there weren't too many of them—as the only legitimate times to lie on your bed and read or while away the hours playing cards.

Camp rain gear from the twenties covered you from head to toe.

Crowds gathered around the best storytellers in camp during rainy-day sessions.

*A wooden Canada goose, with a shingled body, legs of tree trunks, and laminated wooden wings that actually flapped, was constructed for a surprise birthday party for Camp Kehonka's founder, Laura I. Mattoon. Later it served as a float for a Fourth of July parade. The festivities were held up several times, though, so obstructing limbs along the route could be removed.*

# Special Events

"Turtles on your mark. Get set. Go!" The scene was the basketball court for the 1953 running of the traditional turtle race. One reptile from each cabin or tent (that so desired) was trained by a camper/coach—some with great skill evidently, because at the moment the dash began, a number made a beeline for the finish. Unfortunately, crowding campers in a frenzy of excitement frightened many of the contestants, who then retreated. One recalcitrant turtle pulled its head and feet into its shell, and some campers swore they heard "turtilian snores" coming from beneath the lid. However, there was a winner, by the name of Archie, much to the chagrin of Vitesse, Slomoshin Racer, Greased Lightning, and Rabbi Kramer.

Special events could be ridiculous or grandiose, from turtle races to all-day carnivals, but they all had one thing in common: Campers loved them. Part of the appeal was the total surprise start of some of the events. When that announcement at breakfast was heard, campers went wild: "Today is Apache Relay!" Camp was divided into two teams, which spent a hilarious morning performing such feats as shooting baskets, shaving balloons, kindling a campfire, unwrapping twenty individually wrapped raisins from tinfoil and eating them, knitting a row, or scoring a "ten off" at shuffleboard.

Some events began *before* breakfast. For the youngest campers, one special treat was the pajama swim. Awakened at 6:00 A.M., they were marched down to the beach and got to swim in their pj's, which filled up with air like balloons. Only the youngest in camp would think this was neat. The older and wiser campers would rather stay in bed and avoid the cold lake.

Ghost Night occurred after taps at Camp Hiawatha, where loudspeakers woke up campers at what "seemed like 3:00 A.M." Everyone bundled up in bathrobes and blankets and stumbled to the theater for an extremely scary and eerie ghost show.

Mention the clacking of rocks, and most campers will think "snipe." A typical snipe hunt story from Camp Waldron in 1932 involved procuring two young red roosters and doctoring their appearances with extra feathers and topknots, attached, believe it or not, with airplane glue. After stories of Mongolian snipe were spread, fifty-four campers went into the woods after dusk to flush out the critters, yelling and knocking rocks together and on trees. Somehow the idea that they had actually caught these two birds was foisted upon the campers, who dined the next evening on the deliciously cooked Mongolian snipe.

*The favorite booth at any camp carnival was the one where you could douse your counselors, provided your aim with a softball hit the triggering mark.*

One step in an Apache relay—keeping those eggs above water and on the spoons.

Many campers in the West looked forward to a camp rodeo during their stay. At the Cheley Colorado Camps, butting billy goats took the place of bucking broncos.

Another occasion for a special event was the grand old Fourth of July, which could bring patriotic speeches and songs, parades in town (for which camp floats were often built), fireworks displays, pie-eating contests, and traditional games. The Kennebec race started on July 4, 1912, and continues today with few changes. It was essentially an obstacle race, where, if you didn't come in first, you could always brag about coming in last. Campers had to:

Swim seventy-five feet without wetting the flag you hold, dry thoroughly and dress, walk backwards fifty yards and drop the flag in a box tied to the flag pole above your head, crawl under two tent flies nailed to the ground, saw a piece of wood, turn three somersaults at home plate, carry a potato on a board to right field and throw it over the fence.

Camp Wigwam's Water Carnival was an all-day event to which the public was invited. The morning was occupied by canoe and boat races and tilting. In the afternoon, a swim competition was held, as well as a demonstration of life-saving by the Junior Red Cross Corps. After dinner a canoe exhibition was given by the Class A canoeists, who performed such feats as jumping to the gunwales, the kangaroo hop, the head stand, and canoe aquaplaning. Following this was a play, topped off by a Pageant of Lanterns, in which an area of the lake was lit up by lanterns and spotlights. Floats on canoes were designed and constructed by tent groups, and these would be paddled from the dark recesses of the lake into the floodlit area, and back into the dark again, to rounds of applause. In 1925, themes included Japanese tea gardens; Viking ships; a fiery dragon; and the skyline of New York, complete with Dutch windmills.

Some of the most ambitious special events were the circuses and carnivals. For weeks before the big day, groups would meet to plan their booths, sideshows, games, and entertainment. Costumes were dug out of trunks and clown makeup daubed on to anyone who wanted it. At the magic moment the midway opened, the barkers barked, the hawkers hawked, and the show began.

A Depression-era float at Camp Wigwam's Water Carnival commented on the times.

In 1924, Camp Greylock began a long tradition of putting on an annual circus, "a project so gigantic that hitherto it had not been attempted." As at many camps, all proceeds from admission and booths along the midway were donated to charity.

*Visitor's Day is a great excuse for taking pictures. This is only a part of one family's documentation: posing with tentmates, posing with Dad, and posing with Mom. There were also snapshots of Mom in front of the tent, the baseball game, and the picnic.*

# Visitor's Day

Kids that couldn't wait to leave their parents at the beginning of the summer couldn't wait to see them on Visitor's Day. Waiting anxiously for your parents to drive in, you ran down in your mind your agenda for the big day: You'd show off how you could get up on one ski (hoping your father had brought the movie camera along); you'd present them with the hammered copper tray you'd just finished at arts and crafts; you'd regale them with the full details of the three-day canoe trip you'd only mentioned in a postcard home.

When the big moment arrived, campers were smothered with hugs and kisses and, sometimes, contraband food. At Kennebec, parents' cars used to be known as "fruit wagons" but often contained more than just fruit. One counselor, suspecting ice cream was being smuggled into camp by some parents, kept them in conversation just long enough to make sure it melted.

Occasionally parents arrived with a splash. Many camps have seen the odd seaplane land on the lake and taxi right up to the beach. One summer the family of a camper actually arrived on camp grounds in a helicopter. What's more, they were attired in space suits and amazed onlookers further by throwing Mars candy bars to the kids.

After arrival, parents were paraded around camp to meet counselors, see the bunk, and meet friends. Usually the camp was on its best behavior, but slipups did occur. The story was told from 1950, of a "brawny" counselor dashing into his cabin after a dip on Visitor's Day. After stripping down, giving himself "a vigorous rubdown," and dressing, he realized, to his utter shock, that he had not been alone. At one end of the cabin a mother had been having a quiet conversation with her son. The counselor bolted outdoors and avoided the parent until departure time. At that point she found him and with no explanation gave him five dollars while shaking hands.

Usually the entertainment was more planned—parent-camper ball games or swimming meets, theatrical productions, barbecues, or regular activities with parents looking on.

If you were lucky, you were allowed to leave camp with your parents to go out for a meal. But, the rules were pretty strict about what time you had to be back and when your parents had to leave. At the appointed hour, the mass exodus took place, and tearful campers tried to think, once again, more about camp and less about home.

## A MOTHER ONCE CAME UP TO CAMP
*(Tune: "Yankee Doodle")*

*A mother once came up to camp*
*To see her darling daughter,*
*And when she saw how well she swam*
*Said, "Don't go near the water."*

*Chorus:*
*Daughter, daughter, please take care,*
*Your poor mother you will scare,*
*Skill like yours is very rare,*
*Be careful, darling daughter.*

*Daughter, don't play in the sun*
*At basketball or baseball,*
*Or you might bleach your golden hair,*
*Which would not do at all.*

*Chorus:*
*Daughter, don't climb Washington,*
*For when you reach the summit*
*You might trip and stub your toe*
*And then go rolling down it.*

*Chorus*

*This Walden song from the 1920s is still a camp favorite.*

*Camp Lenore had a long-standing tradition of weekly Rituals. In each one a Bible story was acted out in pantomime with accompanying music. In the 1930s girls presented Joseph and his coat of many colors.*

# Usually on Sunday

Traditional religious services were *not* commonplace at camp. If your parents wanted you to go to a camp that incorporated religion into its program, they found a place that advertised that fact. There were many Jewish camps, church camps, and Y camps from which to choose. You could even have your bar mitzvah at camp, if you wanted. And camps plainly stated that transportation was provided to town for Catholics to attend Mass. But for the most part, religion was given the summer off at camp.

Services at camp were usually another matter. Sometimes different bunk units took responsibility each week for the event, putting on a skit, a reading, or a sing-along. Otherwise the director took charge and used the opportunity of having the whole camp captive for a half hour on Sunday to educate the campers on a variety of subjects. Dr. Luther Gulick gave weekly talks in the teens on the following themes: how a girl could develop her vitality under modern city conditions; why there had never been a great team game played by women until that generation; the art of the hostess—an illustration of woman's power; boys.

At times the weekly service was used as a public forum for misbehavers to apologize to camp. In one instance, boys who had not lived up to the values of camp were tapped early on in the week for a very uncomfortable meeting in the director's office to prepare a plan to better themselves. These "plans" were presented before the entire camp at Sunday services in the grove.

Most campers didn't really mind Sundays. To begin with, you were treated to an extra half hour in the sack. "Lazy Sunday" sometimes meant being able to go down to breakfast in your pajamas. Activities also shifted gears, and the camper/counselor ball games always drew a crowd. Of course, at some point during the day you *did* have to trudge off for the weekly get-together.

Former campers tend to remember less what was said in the groves and outdoor chapels than what they experienced during those periods—the quiet break in the week, communing with nature and the outdoors, snapping twigs found on the ground into small pieces, peeling bark off the benches in front of them, and watching a lone ant march the entire length of a bench seat undisturbed.

*A rustic altar with a carpet of leaves provided the focus for the outdoor chapel at Camp Kehonka.*

*Some of the values directors hoped to instill in their campers were conspicuously placed at the entrance gate to Camp Takajo.*

119

*A rousing good campfire at Camp Chewonki.*

# Campfire

*When the pine bough flames on high*
*When Bear Lake drinks down the sky*
*We'll gather round with tuneful sound*
*Some red hot corn to try.*
*Campfire days, campfire days,*
*Cheery old pals around the blaze,*
*Hand in hand, happy band,*
*No one so happy in the land.*

Songs around the campfire were one of the best things about camp. Often written early in the camp's history, almost always by campers or counselors, they were passed on season to season, camper to camper. Something about the campfire brought out the music. Ukuleles, guitars, harmonicas, and accordions appeared as if by magic. The relaxed, informal atmosphere of campers encircling the fire made it easy—almost invited you—to get up and perform. By the end of the summer, even the most reticent had attempted a solo song or a ghost story.

Songs about camp formed the nucleus of the musical fare around the campfire. There were the sentimental odes that extolled the glories of camp: the lake, the trees, the secluded site, and the camp family. The fight songs were snappier and louder but not necessarily more popular. These were augmented by folk songs, show tunes, and even popular songs of the day. Some of these became such favorites that they were accorded the honor of being entered into the camp songbooks.

The campfire was an event always looked forward to. It was packed with tradition, which began with the laying of the fire itself. Often it was built "four-square," and at Camp Greylock this solemn and sober tradition was explained: The four corners stood for Fortitude, Beauty, Truth, and Love. In the twenties, different clubs at camp competed against one another to build the best campfire, and "as a result they were always symmetrical and sturdy."

Campfire was usually held one night a week—less often than most campers would have wanted it. Frequently the brand of entertainment wasn't much different than an evening program in the lodge or theater. But being huddled around the campfire made it different. If you weren't too interested in what was being presented, you could always stare into the glowing embers.

The performances at campfires, by counselors and campers alike, were widely and wildly varied, and equally entertaining. Beyond the group singing, which got it all off to a rousing and

*Building a fire as big as you are, in the 1920s.*

### CAMPFIRE FOR JUNIORS

The whole Junior Camp went up to Campcraft to have a campfire on the night of August 7, 1980.

Once we came in we sat on logs and watched as Paul set the fire. At first it wouldn't spread, then he got a Kleenex box and boy did it spread!

Well, we sang the Mohican song and other funny songs.

Soon it came to the last song. Three kids helped put out the fire with their canteens.

*From the Mah-Kee-Nac Totem.*

*The campfire doesn't have to be a big event. Sometimes it's just an Indian-style cookout for a bunk or two.*

*Often a couple of counselors playing instruments is all a campfire needs.*

energetic start, there was an ever-changing series of individual performances, such as a recitation of "Casey at the Bat," vividly rendered and acted out; a reenactment of the argument between Brutus and Cassius from *Julius Caesar*; highlights of camp history, including the great color war contests, or how the camp was founded (a perennial favorite); and, of course, ghost stories were a must at *every* campfire.

There were standard ghost stories told year after year, embellished somewhat differently with each retelling. A classic from Camp Pemigewassett concerned "the one-armed brakeman." As the story went—and these are only the bare-boned facts— there was once a brakeman on the camp train, which traveled to Fairlee, Vermont. One of the recreations en route to camp was teasing this man and playing pranks on him. At one point a camper pulled the emergency switch and the train screeched to a halt. The unfortunate brakeman was between cars and had an arm cut off when the train lurched forward. The one-armed brakeman swore revenge, and every summer since his ghost has returned to the hills around camp searching for that elusive camper, and scaring the camp population at large.

Campfire was also a celebration of Indian lore. For those camps that went in for it, everything from starting the fire to the last ritual dance, was based on a real or invented Indian prototype. One feature of the Indian council fire at camp was the challenge, or contest, and these games entertained campers at all camps.

The procedure for campfire games in the thirties was rigorously laid out. First there would be an opening event. This was followed by one or two contests, and capped off with "a combat of exciting type." (It could be said that there was little difference among opening events, contests, or combats.) Here's a sampling: There were two favorite opening events from which to choose, face-making and talking contests. In each, two campers got up before the crowd and performed for thirty seconds. At the end of the time, the amount of applause determined the winner and another camper rose to the challenge.

One of the many contests was goat butting, in which two campers got down on their hands and knees and butted volleyballs with their heads only. The first to cross the line with the ball was the winner, and another would challenge. Siamese twins involved two teams of two campers each. The team members would stand back to back, astride a broomstick, each grasping an end. At a signal, they would run the course and back again. First one would run backward and one forward, and then vice versa. Once again the winners would be challenged.

For the final event a combat was staged, often a boxing event wherein the object was to knock the other's hat off. The boxers were prohibited from touching their own hats, no matter how precariously they were perched on their heads.

Aside from fun and games, the campfire was also a mixture of fellowship and friendship, roasted marshmallows, s'mores, and other fireside treats.

The final campfire of each season was different from all the rest. Each camp song had new meaning, as the season was summed up and another one looked forward to.

> If I lived to be nearly a hundred
> And every year one of joy,
> I wonder if I should remember
> The times when, as a boy,
> I sat by the campfire at Pemi
> With a group of the nation's best
> As the moon drifted low o'er the hillside
> And finally dropped in the west.
>
> And I wonder if anyone's better
> For anything I've done or said,
> And whether good will in the heart may
> Offset mistakes of the head.
> Perhaps when life's mem'ries are gathered
> The camp ones will be with the rest
> As the moon drifts low o'er the hillside
> And finally drops in the west.

*Chef's hat boxing was at one time a popular campfire game.*

*Opening wide for a charred marshmallow.*

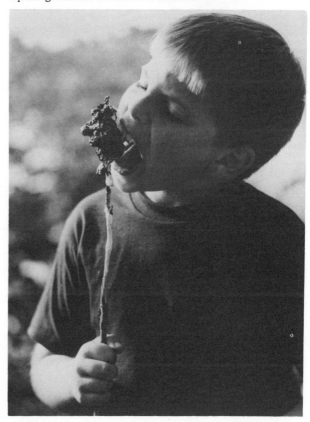

*Mother I like CAMP. I do like CAMP fiere's. We went for one CAMP. fiere's.*

*Hank*

*Postcard home from a six-year-old camper in 1948.*

123

*The Mexican hat dance could be a fun evening activity, even without boys.*

# After Dark

During the hiatus between dinner and dark you usually got to do pretty much whatever you wanted. There was often a pickup softball game on the upper diamond or a highly contested camper/counselor volleyball game going on, and it was a great time to squeeze in a last set of tennis. Some campers were always milling around the lodge waiting for something to happen, while others were calling "winners" at the Ping-Pong table.

All-camp games were a favorite organized after-dinner pastime. One former camper remembered with glee the dinosaur egg hunts. Campers scoured the woods and grounds for "dinosaur eggs," which bore a strong resemblance to watermelons. Everyone could feast on the delicacy, and a prize went to the camper who found the biggest one. It was well deserved, because the heavy "egg" had to be lugged all the way to the lodge for the weigh-in.

The counselor hunt was another activity that took place before dark at many camps. At Camp Winnebago, the boys had one hour to flush the ensconced counselors from their hiding spots. Five counselors were secretly chosen before the hunt to be the prime targets. After the event, the five names were made known. If the unfortunate counselors had been found during the hunt, they were subjected to a series of innocent, but humiliating pranks. (All in the spirit of fun, of course.) If, however, any of them eluded their captors during the allotted hour, they could, in turn, choose another counselor who had been caught to take the medicine instead. Another variation on the outcome occurred at Camp Pemigewassett. There all counselors who were caught had to jump in the lake with their clothes on.

It goes without saying, that after dinner was the perfect time for snipe hunts. Dusk seemed to be the time when snipe were most plentiful on the grounds and just right for bagging.

As darkness approached, an onslaught of hungry mosquitoes sent everyone back to the bunks. Shorts were doffed for long pants. Sweatshirts and a good dose of 6-12 insect repellent completed the change. Then it was off for evening program with flashlight in pocket or hand.

There have always been favorite evening programs. Campers lamented in 1913 that "campfires cannot always be the means for the evening pastime, nor can indoor baseball be the invariable rule for after supper amusement." The campfire, with storytelling and corn and marshmallow roasts, certainly continued as a welcomed activity, whereas the sport of indoor baseball seems to have been lost somewhere down the road.

### EVENING ACTIVITY
### (Tune: "Officer Krupke")

*Evening activity, what will it be*
*Oh hurry up and tell us, we just*
*    can't wait to see*
*Team meeting or movie would*
*    gladden us so*
*And skinny dip if you dare go*
*What a show!*
*Would there be a chance that we'd*
*    have a dance*
*Or free choice to do what you will*
*Tell us quick, the one that you*
*    have picked.*

Camp Tapawingo songbook.

Two girls dressed up and mugged for the camera en route to the evening masquerade ball.

The camp shutterbugs (above) *got the first row in the outdoor theater whenever skits (below) were the evening program. The purpose of this skit may have been to see who could wear the longest and baggiest jeans.*

In the same year, 1913, movies were an occasional nightly diversion. One camp trudged en masse to the nearby town of Harrison, Maine, for the moving pictures at the Grange Hall. When the show was over, they rushed, as always, to the soda fountain to fill up for the hike home. Although the evening out was a success, the trip home over the dark, dusty road was "by no means pleasant as everyone was completely unnerved at the least rustling in the bushes."

Since then, movies once a week, if not more often, became standard procedure almost everywhere. In the 1920s, three reels were shown: a one-reel travelogue followed by a two-reel silent slapstick comedy, with music provided by the camp jazz band. In the fifties, shorts on "World Series Highlights" were followed by B-grade classics such as *It Came from Beneath the Sea.*

For as long as movies have been shown at camp, there has been a tradition of faulty projectors, screens flapping in the wind, and horrible sound. At Kennebec, in the early days, the logs at camp made special mention when the moving pictures were in focus.

Projection problems aside, movies were fun. Lots of times *free* candy was dispensed before showtime. And it was a great opportunity to sit beside your favorite friend of the opposite sex. Even though supervision was always tight, if the movie was good, the counselors could be lax.

In the never-ending search for diversion in evening programs, outside acts were sometimes brought into camp. During a recent summer, a trio of "world champion" Frisbee throwers traveled the camp circuit, staging breathtaking exhibitions while giving a brief, humorous history of the sport. They astounded campers with unbelievable tosses and spectacular catches, often hampered by high winds.

During the 1940s and 1950s, select groups of full-blooded American Indians traveled all over the country to summer camps offering evening programs. In 1957, for fifty dollars, a camp could have Red Dawn, White Eagle, and Little Jumper for a one-night stand. The program featured authentic blanket and hand sign language, and seven dances in thrilling costume, including the Apache Crown Dance, the Cheyenne Shield Dance, and the Old Chieftain's Dance. Red Dawn himself described the event as "our finest showing and the tops in this sort of entertainment."

Other events filled the evening bill on a regular basis. Plays and skits were staged as frequently as twice a week. If you were

## THE SOCIAL SCENE

Undoubtedly the most popular evening entertainment—for those who reached a certain age—was the camp social, or dance. When the bus pulled up, full of thirty boys or girls, usually nobody knew anyone. So, the dance always got off to a slow start, with boys on one side of the room and girls on the other. Then the standard dance tricks were initiated by the counselor-chaperones to try to induce some intermingling. Two concentric circles were formed, one each with girls and boys. When the music started, you walked in opposite directions. When the music stopped, you *had* to dance with the person you were facing. After that was over and everyone had retreated back to their respective sides, the snowball dance was started. This began with one couple on the floor. When the music stopped, each had to find a new partner. The dance continued in this episodic fashion until everyone was dancing.

It wasn't long after this that the new couples tried to sneak off. When the girls from Pinecliffe came to Androscoggin in 1953, "an out-the-door Bunny Hop failed so the campers had to use other means to slip out of the lodge." It was noted in the *Androlog*, that many were successful. Soon there was a larger crowd at Sunset Rock than remained in the lodge.

There were choice places at every camp where couples could hang out: the lower diamond with its dark seclusion; likewise for the rifle range, which also featured mattresses; any spot in the woods would do; and down by the lake could be especially romantic on a moonlit night.

No matter where you went to camp, there were summer romances galore. In co-ed camps, partners were more or less set after a couple weeks into the season. At one camp, the boys were allowed to escort the girls back to their area. The three separate entrances came to represent how advanced the romance was: One was where girls returned alone; another was populated by couples necking; the third was reserved for more serious petting. Needless to say, there was a lot of prestige attached to which entrance you returned through.

It was a little more difficult, if you went to a boys' or girls' camp, to engage in amorous activity. The opportunities just didn't arise, except at socials, which were always so well supervised. But even if you remained in the dance hall, with the music, the company, the food, *and* the chaperones, you could still have a good time.

*Informality was generally the rule at camp socials. The camp uniform was always acceptable attire. Wallflowers (boys or girls) could usually find a counselor to dance with.*

127

*All eyes were glued to the musical duo of clarinet and recorder at Camp Kehonka.*

in the production, you could look forward to a cast party after the show. At Wyonegonic an adaptation of *Tom Sawyer* was performed for the entire camp. The play stretched on and on long enough into the night that a late breakfast was announced for the following morning, to the raucous cheers of the campers. Then, when the audience had dispersed, a huge cake was brought out for the girls to devour.

At one time campers were also put through a weekly regimen of nature lectures, illustrated with glass slides or movies. Since many campers tended to avoid the nature lodge, this was one method of making sure you got some exposure to nature. Although the lectures were always favorably reviewed in camper publications, it's hard to imagine that anyone really liked them.

Music filled many evenings in camp: singing in the lodge or around the campfire, concerts by camp ensembles and orchestras, and recitals by visiting luminaries. Boys at Camp Wigwam were regularly treated to concerts by musicians such as Leopold Gutowsky and Joseph Hoffman, who would come to camp for a vacation of a week or so. In return, they would give one or two concerts to which the public was also invited.

Evenings at Camp Kehonka were often spent at Musicale. Any camper who was bold enough could get up and perform before the whole camp. The performances ran the gamut from well-rehearsed choruses to a group of girls who went on a trip and wrote a comic ditty about it; or from a very squeaky solo on a recorder to a not-so-squeaky wind ensemble. There was a tradition at the camp of not applauding each individual performance, because more squeaks might have garnered less applause. Instead, you sat on your hands and delivered appropriate pats on the back later. But the system usually broke down after a tremendous performance, when the audience couldn't refrain from bursting into tumultuous applause.

A less formal program, but one campers liked just as much, was game night. Everyone gathered in the lodge with board games, jacks, and playing cards and teamed up for the action. If you couldn't live without the favorite games you'd left at home, you could always write to have your mom send them. One letter from a camper in 1954 contained a dual message:

Dear Mom and Dad, My tooth came out. So I'll send it to you. Please send money. I would like you to send me thease games, Ramar of the Jungle and Uncle Wiggly.

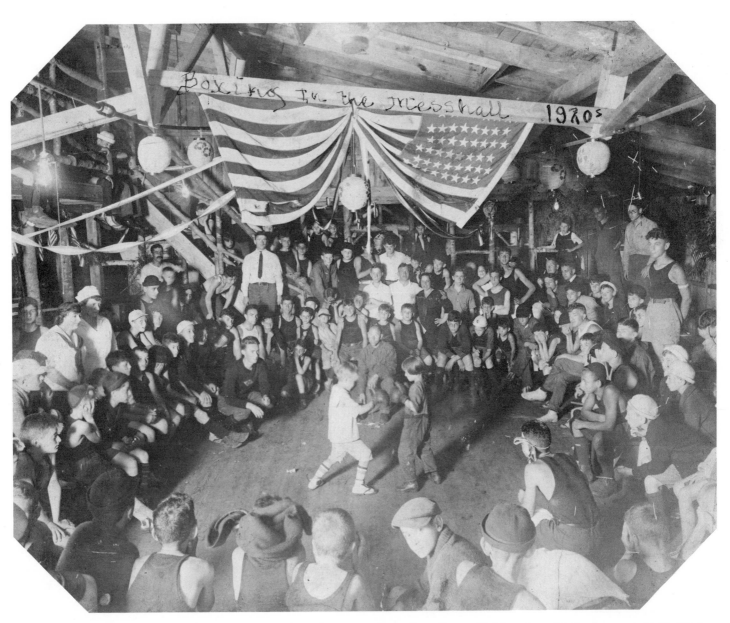

Although boxing was at one time a favorite evening activity, there were always those that couldn't bear to watch the fray, and shielded their eyes against it.

*Two after-dark events in "evening clothes"—girls in pj's
(above) gathered in the lodge for jacks, while boys,
similarly attired (below), enjoyed a well-organized pillow
fight with blindfolded contestants.*

Other game nights depended less on boards and more on group action. Boxing was a long-time favorite, enjoyed one night a week in the lodge or in an outdoor ring. Pillow fights, whether organized or not, created rollicking good fun. And then there were always the likes of dodge ball and "keep away" and "pursuing the potato." This latter contest was described in 1917 as "the ancient and time honored pastime of chasing wild potatoes, popularly known as 'micks,' about the slippery and elusive floor of the lodge." Camp was divided into teams, and each camper was given a soup ladle with which to retrieve the "recalcitrant potatoes." Within the allotted time period, the team that had gently yet firmly deposited the most into a waiting receptacle was declared the winner.

Eventually the fun had to end, and it was time for the crossed-arm singing of the good-night song and taps. Then it was back to the bunk to get ready for bed . . . or ready for action. It was a well-known fact that most horseplay took place under the cover of darkness.

The stillness that counselors tried in vain to enforce was broken by the familiar sound of a ripping sheet, when a camper jumped into a bed that had been "Frenched" or short-sheeted. This particular camp tradition went on for a long time. In the early twenties, they were known as "pie-beds," with variations on the theme being "fancy pie-beds," filled with moss, rocks, or frogs.

It was all downhill from there. At regular intervals cabin units were on the prowl, raiding other bunks, starting pillow fights, or instigating some other mischief.

Almost every camp had, in its history, the story of the sleeper so sound, he or she was carried in bed and set afloat on a raft in the lake without ever waking. There was also the familiar story of the counselor returning from a day off to find an empty spot where her bed had been. It had been hidden by her dear little charges and might have been anywhere, from under the cabin to on the lake.

More daring stunts were carried out against the establishment. Some directors, with their good sense of humor, almost invited the campers to try to top last year's prank. One morning at Camp Dudley, the director found a canoe in his office. This wouldn't have been so bad, except for the fact that it was filled to the gunwales with water. Another year a horse greeted him. That wasn't so bad either; it was what the horse left behind in the office that was disconcerting.

Many campers were known to untie the boats from their moorings, knowing they'd drift across the lake by morning. Running counselors' bras up the flagpole was also standard prank procedure. One former camper commented that the first condom he ever saw was in the form of a funny-shaped white balloon at the top of a flagpole at camp.

Not all horseplay was mischievous. Some was just innocent fun. At one camp word would go out that a "latrine show" was planned for that night. After counselors were asleep, girls would sneak off to the latrine with their flashlights. There two girls at a time would dance or act, while the others shook their flashlights up and down to create an old-time movie effect. The show would go on until their giggling gave them away.

At Camp Somerset, "kidnapping" was a legitimate posttaps activity, in which an older girls' cabin made off with a group of younger girls. "One evening we got kidnapped. . . . They took us all over camp with pillow cases over our heads. They made us walk in mushy mud and they picked up and twirled us. Then they took us to their bunk, and we had popcorn, punch, and s'mores. We had tons of fun."

Occasionally, what started out as an innocent prank backfired. A former camper from Camp Owaissa wanted to create Christmas in July. She and a friend spent hours one night covering many of the trees around camp with soap flakes. The following morning the results looked spectacular, but their glee turned to horror when they were told the soap would kill the trees. They fessed up and spent the entire day hand washing the soap from every leaf.

Given the infinite variety and severity of capers at camp, it's no wonder that when people reminisce about their summer days, the first things that are brought to mind are the outstanding pranks pulled off.

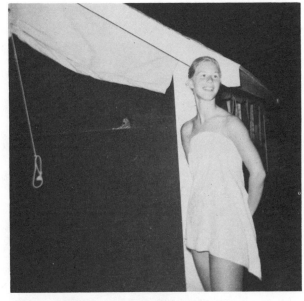

*A nighttime skinny-dipper returns to her cabin, hoping she has not been seen by anyone but her friends.*

*This bed and trunk, under the cabin, may be hard to see during the daylight. Imagine the counselor returning at night from her day off and trying to locate them. Successful pranks against counselors were lauded by campers and counselors alike.*

*Exact positioning; perfect posture; two motionless teams compete for song and cheer. The slightest movement out of line could be grounds for point loss.*

# Color War!

Dear Mom + Dad, Last night it started! I'll tell you about it later. I don't have much time now. I'm on the Red. Right now we are up by a quarter of a point.

Color War! That time-honored, long-standing tradition of dividing camp into two teams of equal ability, each named after one of the camp colors. Three to five days of intense competition on land and water, in the dining hall, in the lodge, and in the cabins.

Everyone knew it would happen during the last weeks of camp, but no one knew exactly when it would start—and it always started with a bang. Not only that, but often there would be a false start or two, to heighten the tension. These were very dramatic; for example, a low-flying airplane buzzed the camp, dropping hundreds of leaflets in the camp colors, all announcing, "This is *not* the start of color war."

The actual beginning could be heralded by fire engines screaming into camp; a seaplane pulling up to the beach; visiting girls from a sister camp stripping to bikinis in the team colors; or as subtle as ribbons in camp colors tied to cots under the cover of darkness.

One of the more shocking starts occurred at Camp Wigwam in 1962. During the usual predinner announcements, an argument began between the director and a popular counselor. Within minutes, the incident escalated to the point where the director gave the counselor his walking papers and told him to start packing. With that, the counselor drew a gun and, to the horror of the entire camp, fired a round at the director, who fell back, a red stain of ketchup appearing on his shirt. At that point, the arts and crafts counselor ran onto the scene, bedecked in red and gray, and it all became clear.

Once it had begun, color war took over every aspect of camp. The goal, simply enough, was to amass more points than your opponents. All life was governed by the awarding of points for victories and the deducting of points for infractions.

Athletic contests were do or die. The best athletes in each age group competed for the precious points in all endeavors. There were also usually two all-camp relay races, one in track and one in the water, where everyone, regardless of ability or inclination, had to participate.

If you weren't in a competition or practicing for one, you were expected to be in attendance somewhere, cheering your team on. A typical period was jam-packed as follows: 10:45 to 11:30—Senior basketball (large court); Intermediate tennis

*Cheerleading the Red team on to victory in a legendary, one-twelfth of a point win over the Grays at Camp Wigwam in 1954.*

*Camper hygiene is parodied in the* Totem Pole *during color war.*

(upper courts); Junior 2 archery; Junior 1 riflery; Cub riflery; Junior 3 archery.

It usually happened that the best athletes in each event were on opposite teams. Therefore, color war was also a time to determine, once and for all, who was top dog: who was the best tennis player in camp, the best archer, the best pitcher. . . . Sometimes the contests became part of the camp folklore, taking on a significance beyond color war. One story was often repeated of a 1950s' color war tennis match at Camp Wigwam, in which the two top Senior players were pitted against each other. Courtside was packed for the showdown. In the middle of the contest, one of the players, in going back for a lob, smashed into the wire fence. His collision dislodged the horizontal log on the top of the fence, which careened down upon him and knocked him unconscious. Play was interrupted until the camper was brought to but then resumed promptly. It was play or lose . . . and he did both, played *and* lost. In color war, headache or no, you don't forfeit a game. For once, the better tennis player could not be fairly determined by the outcome. The more gung-ho player was clearly evident.

Off the athletic field, competition was just as stiff. In fact, it began before reveille—no camper could arise earlier. "Violations of this rule will be considered serious. One-half point for each infraction."

The teams assembled and marched in columns of twos to the lodge for flag-raising. This performance was worth three points and was judged on promptness, straightness of the line, cleanliness, and neatness of the campers.

During color war you sat by team in the dining hall. Often, no points were awarded for meals, but quarter points could be deducted for any infractions, including poor table manners. The teams were controlled by hand signals—when to sit, when to stand, when to march.

It was cabin and tent inspection, though, that instilled fear in every camper's heart. Points that you earned so dearly on the athletic field—an entire baseball game being worth only five points—could disappear like lightning if your cleanup was slipshod. A lumpy blanket folded at the foot of your bed: one-quarter point deduction. Sneakers not properly aligned under the cot: one-quarter point. Toothpaste spatters on the mirror: one-quarter point. Cupboard door left ajar: one-quarter point. The possibilities were endless.

Similarly, rest hour was another struggle. Each camper had

A variety of unusual games took place only during color war, and often involved the entire camp. Three such games were the hoop race, the tug of war, and an elaborate basketball shooting contest where the shooter had to make a basket, go to the head of the line, and roll the ball backward through the legs of his teammates. The last one in line then shot.

The Brown team formation in 1961 at Hiawatha was an anchor to symbolize strength. Unlike precision marching bands at football halftime, color war teams had the benefit of chalk lines on the lodge floor.

### YOU TAKE THE PEP
*(Tune: "We Are the Girls")*

*You take the pep from a bowl of Wheaties*
*You take the smile from Dentyne gum*
*You take the skin from a Woodbury facial*
*And for a sunny disposition take a Tum*
*And when you put them all together*
*With a swish and a swirl of a curl*
*You have standing there before you*
*A typical Blue Team girl.*

Camp Tapawingo songbook.

### BROWN TEAM SONG
*(Tune: "Thunderation")*

*Bruno showed creation*
*And invented Brown Team nation*
*Energy, determination*
*Gave us quite a reputation*

*Unity is the foundation*
*For this mighty Brown Team nation*
*We have got the spiritation*
*To create a big sensation. . . .*
*Yeah, Browns!*

Camp Walden, 1965.

136

to remain on the bed, quietly, with shoes off, for the entire period. One-quarter point for each violation.

There were lots of other ways your team score could be whittled down. A compulsory swim twice a day was fine for those who liked the water. Those who stayed away cost the team one-quarter point. "Failure to keep warm" was another infraction described in the 1930s.

Poor sportsmanship was especially costly: swearing on the field of competition, two points; heated arguments with team-mates, contestants, or officials, one or two points; striking an official or opponent, five points and possible disqualification from color war.

Sure, you had to be careful about losing points. However, you also had to continually win points in order to beat your opponents.

One of the "high stakes" events came the final night of color war: song and cheer competition. As many as one hundred points were up for grabs, to be divided however the judges saw fit. Each team had to compose an original song and an original cheer and perform them, along with a designated camp song. The only accompaniment allowed was piano. The original works were totally committed to memory, and these were known to run as much as fifty-nine lines long. Practices were held in fits and spurts throughout the color war. When the big night arrived, each team was immaculately attired and groomed. In 1929, at Camp Somerset, girls were described as having, "each shoelace tied with geometric precision, each bloomer pleat standing out with almost unnatural pertness, each lock of hair subdued to the $n^{th}$ degree of lady-like modesty." Campers with especially bad voices were instructed to mouth the words only. The performances were judged on originality, theme, projection, and cleverness.

All the hours of practice and memorization were put to the test. Each team was signaled by hand to rise silently, as if one person. Then, as near a flawless performance as possible was given. The teams traded off, song for song, cheer for cheer. Wonder and excitement at the other team's creations added to the intensity of the evening. And when it was all over, and the judges had made their decisions, not only had the results of the song and cheer been decided, but the final tally of color war as well. Pure bedlam broke loose and hysteria took over. A round of "Auld Lang Syne" ended the evening, and the fray, for another year.

### RED TEAM ORIGINAL CHEER

*Now listen all, now listen well*
*To this tale we have to tell*
*A tale that tells of many deeds,*
*Of all the virtues Gray Team needs.*
TEAMWORK! TEAMWORK! TEAMWORK!
*To illustrate this last remark*
*Here's a sample for a start.*
*When we march, we march with vim.*
*When we fight, we fight to win.*
SPIRIT! SPIRIT! SPIRIT!
*If we should ever fall behind,*
*Then Gray must know that they will find*
*When chips are down we still come through*
*Because of Red Team spirit true.*
FRIENDSHIP! FRIENDSHIP! FRIENDSHIP!
*You'll find the Gray Team to admit*
*That Red Team leads in comradeship*
*For though we rarely lose a game*
*We always act in friendship's name.*
ATHLETICS! ATHLETICS! ATHLETICS!
*On the land we do excell*
*In the lake we do as well*
*Land or lake, we are the best*
*Red Team stands above the rest.*
LOYALTY! LOYALTY! LOYALTY!
*The most important thing of all*
*Is loyalty to one and all*
*Feeling close to one another*
*Reds will not betray a brother.*
TEAMWORK! SPIRIT! FRIENDSHIP!
ATHLETICS! LOYALTY!
*The sum of all these five parts*
*Will live in all the Red men's hearts*
*For in the 50th year of camp*
*The Red Team proved to be the champ.*

*Camp Wigwam, 1960.*

### TAN TEAM SONG
*(Tune: "Put Another Nickel In")*

*T and A and N and S*
*Thanks to Tango's eagerness*
*Has spelled the Tan Team with success*
*And victory, victory, victory.*

*T and A and N and S*
*Spirit at its very best*
*From North, East, South, and West*
*We've got the Tan Team, Tan Team,*
*Tan Team!!!*
*Camp Walden, 1965.*

### GRAY TEAM ORIGINAL CHEER

*Red Team listen, hear your fate*
*You've lost the fight,*
*You're much too late!*

*On the field your big Red men*
*Towards Vict'ry fought, and then—*
*And then, what happened Red?*
*Why did you lose?*
*What are the reasons for your blues?*

*You started back at riflery,*
*Where one frail heart sealed destiny;*
*Tennis, swimming, speed and ball—*
*Gray Team spirit won them all!*

*To earn the glory takes a hand*
*Who'll fight as one on lake or land.*
*Though one man cannot win alone,*
*United teams bring vict'ry home!*

*With all these strikes against you, Red,*
*You couldn't hope to get ahead*
*So Red Team know your doom is nigh*
AS GRAY TEAM LIFTS ITS FLAG ON HIGH!

*Camp Wigwam, 1962.*

*Twice each summer, the entire population of campers at Sebago-Wohelo is towed in a procession of the camp's fleet of boats. This picture is from their Water Sports Day in 1940.*

*A camp without tradition*
*Is like a game without a team,*
*Is like a kid without camp spirit*
*Is like a book without a theme.*

*A day without some fun had*
*Is like our lake without a moon,*
*Is like a trip without a counselor,*
*Is like a song without a tune.*

*So it's up to us at Walden*
*To make tradition last,*
*To form a stronger tie*
*With the years gone by,*
*As it has been in the past.*

This Camp Walden song from the early forties (to the tune of "A Man Without a Woman") tried to embody that intangible camp phenomenon: the sense of tradition. From the first camp songs sung on the train en route, to the tearful farewell banquet, the entire season was steeped in tradition.

In the compressed time frame of camp—you spent only a fixed number of weeks over a limited number of summers—the second time something happened, it was "traditional." New traditions were continually added to camp lore, to augment those dating back to the very beginnings of the camp.

To initiate new campers to life at camp, traditional pranks were sometimes played, in which the whole camp gladly took part. Unexpectedly each summer, unsuspecting, seemingly healthy newcomers to Camp Dudley invariably developed a case of "ear lobes," usually attributed to the icy waters of Lake Champlain. Older campers were always the first to spot the terrible affliction, and they sent the patients straight off to the infirmary, where tincture of iodine was painted on the diseased lobes, at once curing them and marking the boys as first-timers.

Another tradition geared toward the uninitiated was described in the 1930s by the director of Camp Belnap in New Hampshire. At the end of the first Woodcraft Circle Meeting of the summer, the spirit of Chief Masqua (legendary leader of the camp) was invoked, "Come and reign over us tonight, O Chief." With that the storyteller and the campers all looked upward at the sky. Meanwhile, someone away from the group with a fire extinguisher sent a spray of water on high. As the drops landed on the uplifted faces, the storyteller rebuked, "Not rain *on us,*

*This raft, hauled into the lake and set on fire, marks a traditional end to the 1980 season at Camp Androscoggin.*

C is for cramps which we have in the back
from bending for beans of which there's no lack.

A 's for ambidextrous, a quality needed
especially when gardens have to be weeded.

M is for manpower of which there's no dearth
constant care of the stables has shown us its worth.

P 's for the price paid by giving up cups
so small Russian children could have bigger sups.

R is for rows in the vegetable garden
which always need tending and make muscles
harden.

U is for utensils from every meal
which are washed without groans 'cause dishpan
hands heal.

N is for knitting if you leave off the K
mittens and afgans were made that way.

O is for oomph with which everything's done
working, athletics, and all kinds of fun.

I 's for infirmary which needn't be used
if care is taken and limbs aren't abused.

A is for allegiance to our country first of all
and you, as campers, have answered the call.

*The logs at Camp Runoia are filled not only with camp anecdotes, but history as well. This entry from 1943 reflects on the changed lifestyle of camp during a war year.*

Masqua, reign over us." Part of the camp spirit of Belnap meant getting rained on every year, even though you knew it was coming, rather than spoil it for the new campers.

At Camp Pemigewassett a long-standing tradition was recently changed. Originally, all new campers were encouraged to whittle a soup spoon for "bean soup" at the end of the first week in camp. All week long, busy hands worked at carving a spoon from a single piece of wood. At the end of the week, the entire camp gathered for *Bean Soup,* which, rather than being a delectable comestible, was the name of the camp log that was read aloud each week. Naturally, the joke was on the carvers. Nowadays, anyone who so desires can whittle a spoon for a carving contest, which has supplanted the original hoax.

The weekly reading of camper logs was a time-honored tradition at many camps. The daily events were chronicled by a different camper each day. At camps such as Runoia and Alford Lake, the many volumes of logs, written longhand in both poetry and prose, provide a goldmine of their camps' histories.

Some traditions were very small and low-key. They could even start by accident. At Camp Walden, where vociferous singing was one of the salient features of camp life, there was always a tradition of song leading. Until 1922, the song leaders would conduct in unison, using two hands. In that fateful year, one of the girls suffered a broken arm, and since then all song leading has been done with one arm only.

The Bat was first spotted around the Winona Camps in 1908. Several times each summer since then, a counselor in cape and mask presented himself fleetingly to unsuspecting campers. Popping out of laundry baskets, swinging from trees, or running through the dining hall, when the Bat made his surprise appearances, the campers tried to catch him. If one succeeded, the prize was a free summer at camp, but the Bat has never been caught yet.

Beyond the fun and games of fooling the new campers or chasing a counselor dressed as a bat, there were the more sober traditions. The highlight of the season at Camp Waldemar in Texas was the Ideal Girl Ceremony, eagerly anticipated all summer long. It was strived for by every girl in camp, because the Ideal Girl trophy represented the sweetest, most honest, and unselfish camper. She was selected by the whole camp and staff, and the presentation of her coveted award was made at a candlelight ceremony at the end of the season. Former Ideal

Girls from many years past returned to camp just to take part in the event. After the announcement was made, they paddled the current winner down the Guadalupe River in a white canoe while the rest of the camp sang a tear-choked song in her honor.

There was also a strong oral tradition at all camps. The opening and closing campfires were the same every year, with the same stories and legends retold around them time and again. Each summer the campers were reminded of the historic moment the camp began, how it fortuitously came to be located on its present site, the awe-inspiring legends of the surrounding hills, and unbelievable tales of prowess of the early campers and counselors.

At Camp Wigwam a totem pole carved by a counselor illustrated the story of nearby Bear Mountain and how it got its name, and this tale was related every summer. Many moons ago four Indian children were playing when a bear came upon them. Their screams frightened the bear into the lake and also brought their parents to the scene. By this time, the bear had swum the lake and was climbing the mountain on the opposite shore. The frantic father hurled a gigantic tomahawk at the bear but missed him. The force of the tomahawk split the mountain, and this crack is visible to this day. The lake and the mountain still carry the bear's name.

Frequently the naming of a building around camp became a legend. At Belnap the boys decided the infirmary should have an Indian name, so A-Keest-O-Mac was proposed and agreed to by all. If by slip of the tongue a new camper pronounced it "Achey Stomach," he was reprimanded by the older campers and reminded in no uncertain terms that only the Indian pronunciation was acceptable.

The longer a camp was in existence, the more steeped in tradition it became. With stories and songs passed from fathers to sons and mothers to daughters, old campers to young campers, the continuum is complete. Campers from thirty years ago can revisit camp and hear the same songs being sung and the same cheers being cheered. They can sing and cheer unabashedly and join crossed arms to end the evening with the good-night song. It's only natural to be a camper when at camp.

*One of Camp Waldemar's Ideal Girls clings to her trophy after the traditional, emotion-packed ceremony.*

*City clothes and suitcases made their appearances for the final ride out of camp. All the camp vehicles were pressed into service to handle the crowds and meet timetables.*

# End of the Season

At last they came . . . those final days. Whether you wished for them or wished them away, they were as inevitable as school in September. The very thought that camp would end brought forth the first rivers of tears. Boys might have tried to hide them, but girls cried uncontrollably. One former camper recalled the intense emotionalism: "Our good-byes were so incredibly dramatic . . . sobbing and flailing around."

Especially at girls' camps, much of the last week was spent doing rounds of visits from bunk to bunk, collecting addresses and promising to write (promises generally unfulfilled). Another girl told of crying so hard while autographing campmates' tennis shoes, T-shirts, and memory books, that her turgid face was likened to an overripe tomato.

At some camps the days before departure were reserved for extra-special activities. A jacks tournament took place at Alford Lake Camp to counteract any depression that was setting in. The tradition at Kennebec was that the First Section boys (the oldest ones in camp) assumed the role of counselors. While the campers amused themselves with inspecting for the messiest tent, holding a "bathing ugly" contest, and partaking in unceremonious ceremonies at the washhouse, the real counselors were freed up to dismantle the waterfront and otherwise begin to put the camp to bed for the winter. Traditionally, First Section Day at Kennebec was a turnabout day, with wake-up to taps, followed by breakfast fare that resembled dinner.

In the meantime, everyone in camp was supposed to be busy packing. City clothes, if any, were retrieved from the cedar closets in the lodge and aired out for the return trip home. Trunks were dumped out and half-heartedly cleaned. All possessions were checked to see if by any chance they'd jibe with the list pasted in the lid of the trunk. Items loaned to friends had to be rounded up, if at all possible. After eight weeks, few would still have what they originally brought to camp. Letters home could help account for some of the missing items: "Billy threw my Phillies cap down the falls. He said he would pay me for it." "Kevin wears the same size shoes as I do, so yesterday I traded with him. I gave him my desert boots and I used his engineer boots. They are really neat and he says they keep the snow and rain out real well."

A final trip down to the paddle house was in order to collect your canoe paddle. Crafts projects had to be picked up. The ones you actually wanted to keep had to be padded safely. Then

Tune: "Oh Susannah"

*I came to Camp Kehonka all run down and under-*
*weight.*
*I could not row, I could not swim,*
*I could not dive in straight.*
*My blood was thin, my eyes were dim,*
*In fact I was a sight.*
*My cheeks were pale, just like a ghost—*
*Kehonka put me right.*

*Chorus*
*Oh, Kehonka, that's the place to be*
*For the happy months of summer,*
*Come and spend them there with me.*

*I will go home at the end of camp*
*Refreshed and wide-awake;*
*My skin is tanned, my body strong,*
*I can swim across the lake,*
*I can climb up rocky mountains,*
*I can go from morn to night.*
*All winter long I'll be strong,*
*Kehonka put me right!*

*Chorus*

*When I go home, my fond parents*
*Won't know their darling daughter.*
*For their feeble child no longer whines,*
*"No, no, I hadn't oughter."*
*My buxom, blithe and robust strength,*
*My clothes that are too tight*
*Are only indications how*
*Kehonka put me right!*

*Chorus*

*Camp Kehonka, 1931.*

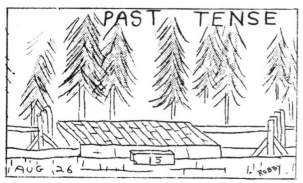

*Few campers got to see the knocked-down camp; but the cartoonist from the 1961* Totem Pole *had a pretty good idea what it would look like.*

🌲 🌲 🌲 🌲 🌲 🌲 🌲 🌲 🌲 🌲 🌲

WHAT THE ABSENT-MINDED CAMPER
WILL DO AND SAY WHEN SHE GETS HOME

1. Throw her napkin away.
2. Remove her spoon from her fruit dish.
3. Get into bed, trying not to push the covers down too far, to try and avoid making it over in the morning.
4. Cheer for ice cream when it is brought to the table.
5. Pile the dishes and push the plates aside.
6. Go to the kitchen for second helpings.
7. Sing camp songs after each course.
8. Rush to the table, in order to get a seat.
9. Wait for the breakfast bugle to blow to get dressed.

🌲 🌲 🌲 🌲 🌲 🌲 🌲 🌲 🌲 🌲 🌲

Somer = Settings, *volume 1, number 8, 1928.*

*A camper recorded the debris with his box camera as airing out preceded the big packup in 1919. The items strewn about had to match the list pasted on the inside of the trunk lid, or you'd have some explaining to do to your mother.*

It is getting to be the end of the year, and everybody is packing. The people's parents who didn't come up are probably glad they are going home now and they can't wait to pack.

We can't make any more projects in Manual Arts or Arts and Crafts because we must pack.

In our cabin Sunday we started to pack. Dick got the trunks down from the rafters. Ned and I and Sheldon wanted to go up with him on the rafters but we couldn't.

So we started to pack things in our trunks, but our counselors told me not to put anything in the trunk. He told us to clean everything out of our closets and put it on the bed. He said that he would give something to every person in the tent after we finished packing. He gave it to Ned before—an Eagle Scout belt, and he gave it to us afterward.

Everybody is anxious to get home. They are running around like mad, and are getting up before reveille and discussing it.

It's only one thing we have to do after we finish packing and that is putting on the tags.

I'm sort of glad that I'm going—but I'm sort of not.

Totem Pole, *August 27, 1951.*
                                                    —Buddy Shushan

came the stuffing of the trunk. Muddy shoes went in first, followed by stuck-together raincoats, dirty clothes, and torn shirts. You were told to put any wet items in a plastic bag, but there wasn't ever a plastic bag around when you needed one. (Perhaps that was why one camp director forewarned mothers to always open trunks in the garage or outside, *never* in the house.) Your duffel bag was left until morning to throw in the last of your bedding and whatever else absolutely wouldn't fit in the bulging trunk.

The final night in camp was the most memorable one. A special campfire with sentimental remembrances of the summer was followed by a subdued ceremony in some camps. At camps Andover-Waldron, the campers slowly carried lit candles, shielded from the breeze, from the campfire to the nearby waterfront. There they were placed on two large floating letters, *A* and *W*. The letters, lit by the candles, were towed out into the lake for the campers to reflect upon until the last light went out.

At Camp Ocoee in Tennessee, the solemn night of the final campfire was called Decision Night. Each camper made a decision or goal about his life and wrote it on a piece of paper. These scraps of paper were then tossed into the fire, the contents known only to the camper.

Hoy Night was the name given to the final bonfire and awards ceremony on the island of Camp Androscoggin. In the 1937 *Androlog* it was described as "the saddest and yet the happiest night of Camp, when a certain something binds you with its spell, so that you can never forget it." The boys spent a major part of the last week dragging in scrap wood and downed branches for the giant bonfire, which was ten to twenty feet high, and was topped that year with two halves of a broken canoe. As the inferno raged, the campers feasted on sandwiches, corn, cantaloupe, and ice cream, and trophies and awards presentations were intermingled with skits and songs.

The eats at Hoy Night, 1937, were pretty good but didn't compare to the banquet menu two years earlier at nearby Camp Somerset for girls: appetizers, fruit cup, consommé, filet mignon, potato chips, peas and carrots, lettuce and tomato salad, ice-cream cake, demitasse, nuts, and mints.

Even though the farewell dinner was usually the best meal of the summer, it was hard to get it down past the lump in your throat. Anyway, it was the awards presentation that followed that the campers most looked forward to. Athletes were honored

*The final campfire was always the saddest one.*

*The final banquet was a time for toasting the successes and mishaps of the season.*

*All who had made the swim across the lake were treated to immortality at the end of the season, on a painted plaque hung in the lodge at Camp Takajo.*

with letters. Achievements in riflery, archery, swimming, and water-skiing were rewarded with numerous patches and medals. Then there were the best camper awards: all-around camper, all-around athlete, progress cups, service cups, and camp spirit cups. There were also improvement and most improved awards. In other words, everybody could get something, and most raked in quite a few.

At Awards Night, campers were also honored for longevity. Felt chevrons, one for each year you'd spent in camp, were handed out for your mother to sew on your camp blanket. Sometimes pins were bestowed on those campers who had been coming loyally for five, ten, or more years.

Despite the finality of it all, a spirit of levity was always present at these occasions. At one of the final banquets at Camp Pemigewassett, the infirmary awards were given to the most infirm. A Plague Plaque recognized twenty-nine campers, and three others were designated recipients of the Pain in the Butt Award. Other camps voted on such dubious achievements as the loudest snorer, the noisiest bunk, and the laziest counselor.

After the pins and needles excitement of the awards ceremony, along with a very sappy, tear-jerking speech or two, it was time for the last singing of the good-night song and taps, which signified the end of camp. You ambled back to your cabin in the moonlight and flashlight for that final night, the last cold water wash, and cool night's sleep on the squeaky cot. You whispered in the dark forever that night. The next morning was an anticlimax, getting up at the crack of dawn and leaving to catch buses, trains, and planes. But all thoughts were still with the summer, and many headed off for home saying, "This was it—the best season ever!"

*Dudleyites at the Milk Station in 1919 scanned the horizon for the train that would carry them home and away from camp for another year.*

*See you next year!*

# Photograph Credits

Page 1, title graphic, courtesy *The Camping Magazine*; page xii, girl reading, courtesy Tripp Lake Camp; page 1, piggyback ride, Camp Wigwam, 1962, authors' collection; page 3, title graphic, courtesy *The Camping Magazine*; page 2, the Junior waterfront, 1926, courtesy Camp Greylock for Boys; page 4, Einstein, courtesy Camp Wigwam; application card, courtesy Camp Dudley; page 5, bungalow row, courtesy Camp Tapawingo; singing, Camp Hiawatha, 1954, courtesy Peggy Gutman Sheren; page 7, title graphic, courtesy Velva Sheen; page 6, "Hello, Richard . . . ," authors' collection; page 7, birthday card, courtesy Camp Winona; camp stamps, courtesy Greater Boston YMCA; page 8, calendar, courtesy Greater Boston YMCA; page 10, uniforms, from *Camps and Camping*, Spalding's Athletic Library, 1924; page 11, Tripp Lake outfit list, courtesy Camp Wigwam; page 13, title graphic, courtesy *The Camping Magazine*; page 12, Grand Central Station, 1951, Wide World Photos, Inc.; postcard, 1950, courtesy Hank Gutman; Tripp Lake, courtesy Camp Wigwam; page 13, good-bye kiss, 1959, courtesy Hildy Largman Stoumen; page 14, the lower berth, courtesy Jane Shapiro Baum; train signs, circa 1958, authors' collection; page 15, girls in truck, courtesy Camp Walden; page 16, postcard, 1951, courtesy Hank Gutman; page 17, gateway, Camp Takajo, photograph by Richard J. S. Gutman, 1981; arrival, courtesy Camp Dudley; page 18, signpost, Harrison, Maine, photograph by R.J.S. Gutman, 1981; page 19, girls at station, courtesy Camp Runoia; disembarking, 1917, courtesy Luther Gulick Camps; page 21, title graphic, courtesy Camp Wigwam; page 20, map, 1934, courtesy Tripp Lake Camp; page 21, canoe and cabin, courtesy Camp Kehonka; tent line, 1945, courtesy Camp Kehonka; page 22, Camp Kehonka sign, courtesy Camp Kehonka; Camp Watitoh sign, photograph by R.J.S. Gutman, 1981; girls in W formation, courtesy Camp Walden; page 23, desk and stand, Camp Kehonka, photograph by R.J.S. Gutman, 1981; lodge, Camp Wigwam, circa 1959, photograph by R.J.S. Gutman; stairway, Camp Yawgoog, photograph by R.J.S. Gutman, 1981; bench, Camp Winnebago, photograph by R.J.S. Gutman, 1981; page 24, boy and cabin, Camp Wigwam, 1961, authors' collection; lone tent, Camp Kehonka, photograph by R.J.S. Gutman, 1981; page 25, banners, Camp Kennebec, photograph by R.J.S. Gutman, 1981; fireplace and painting, North Woods Camp, photograph by R.J.S. Gutman, 1981; lodge interior, Wyonegonic Camps,

photograph by R.J.S. Gutman, 1981; page 27, title graphic, courtesy *The Camping Magazine*; page 26, two girls in a cabin, courtesy Camp Runoia; page 27, boys in front of tent, Camp Wigwam, circa 1955, courtesy Charles C. Baum; four boys with counselors, Camp Arcadia, 1949, courtesy Hank Gutman; page 28, covered wagons, 1981, courtesy The Cheley Colorado Camps; wall plaques, Camp Agawam, photograph by R.J.S. Gutman, 1981; page 29, very clean cabin, 1948, courtesy Camp Greylock for Boys; page 30, girls clowning around, Camp Fernwood, courtesy Jane Shapiro Baum; boys in a tent, courtesy Camp Wigwam; page 31, stuffed animal show, courtesy Alford Lake Camp; relaxing in the cabin, courtesy Camp Pemigewassett; page 33, title graphic, courtesy General Mills, Inc.; page 32, lone bugler, 1922, Courtesy Camp Walden; page 33, toothbrush, from *Camping for Boys* by H. W. Gibson (New York: The Association Press, 1911); morning ablutions, courtesy Tripp Lake Camp; setting-up exercises, courtesy Camp Kehonka; page 34, saluting the flag, YMHA Camp, name unknown, circa 1930, courtesy Dr. Paul Rosenberg; saluting in a tent, courtesy Alford Lake Camp; page 35, cartoon, The 1953 *Androlog*, courtesy Camp Androscoggin; lifting a tree, courtesy Camp Unalayee; page 37, title graphic, courtesy Alex Taylor and Company; page 36, baseball team, courtesy Camp Greylock for Boys; girl at bat, Camp Lenore, courtesy Camp Lenore-Owaissa; page 37, boy at bat, courtesy Camp Wigwam; page 38, three lefties, courtesy Camp Wigwam; tennis serve, Camp Kennebec, 1933, courtesy Hildy Largman Stoumen; page 39, volleyball team, courtesy Camp Watitoh; girls' basketball, courtesy Camp Walden; page 41, title graphic, courtesy *The Camping Magazine*; page 40, using rubbing sticks, 1917, courtesy Luther Gulick Camps; getting the spark, 1917, courtesy Luther Gulick Camps; page 41, Camp Indian, Camp Lilliput, 1941, courtesy Nahum Waxman; tepee, courtesy Camp Wigwam; page 42, signal tower, courtesy Camp Pemigewassett; page 43, ghost rocks, Camp Agawam, photograph by R.J.S. Gutman, 1981; girls with paddles, 1917, courtesy Luther Gulick Camps; page 45, title graphic, from *Boy's Book of Snakes* by Percy A. Morris, copyright © The Ronald Press, John Wiley and Sons, Inc.; page 44, girls in nature lodge, courtesy Alford Lake Camp; page 45, door, Camp Pemigewassett, photograph by R.J.S. Gutman, 1981; page 46, netting specimens, courtesy Alford Lake Camp; page 47, petting the billy, courtesy Camp

Watitoh; posing with animals, courtesy Camp Wigwam; boys in nature lodge, Camp Pemigewassett, photograph by R.J.S. Gutman, 1981; page 48, nature trail, courtesy Camp Wigwam; page 49, Wigwam museum, 1924, courtesy Camp Wigwam; canoeists, 1924, courtesy Camp Wigwam; page 51, title graphic, authors' collection; page 50, taking the plunge, courtesy Alford Lake Camp; sunning on the dock, courtesy Camp Watitoh; page 51, boy with nose-plugs, courtesy Camp Bauercrest; postcard, 1950, courtesy Hank Gutman; page 52, the buddy board, courtesy Camp Lenox for Boys; buddies, hands up, courtesy Camp Kehonka; life-saving jump, courtesy Alford Lake Camp; page 53, on the slide, courtesy Camp Kehonka; cross-chest carry, Camp Somerset, 1932, courtesy Mildred Largman Gutman; miniature skinny-dippers, courtesy Hildy Largman Stoumen; page 54, jackknife, courtesy Camp Kennebec; boys on beach, courtesy Camp Bauercrest; page 55, learning to breathe, courtesy Camp Yawgoog; paddleboards, 1954, courtesy Camp Greylock for Boys; page 57, title graphic, from *The Archery Workshop* by L. E. Stemmler; page 56, touché, courtesy Camp Greylock for Boys; page 57, bowmen, Junior archery, 1938, courtesy Camp Winona; riflery instruction, 1981, courtesy The Cheley Colorado Camps; page 58, on the beam, courtesy Alford Lake Camp; golfing, courtesy Camp Runoia; page 59, quoits, 1954, courtesy Camp Greylock for Boys; sparring partners, Camp Arcadia, 1948, courtesy Hank Gutman; page 61, title graphic, courtesy Camp Waldemar; page 60, riding in the ring, 1981, courtesy The Cheley Colorado Camps; page 61, trail ride, 1981, courtesy The Cheley Colorado Camps; page 62, the packhorse, 1981, courtesy The Cheley Colorado Camps; girls' horseback riding class, courtesy The Wyonegonic Camps; page 63, petting the horse, courtesy Camp Walden; taking a jump, courtesy Camp Wicosuta; leading the trail ride, courtesy Camp Tapawingo; page 65, title graphic, courtesy General Foods Corp.; page 64, girls at table, courtesy Camp Runoia; page 65, postcard, 1951, courtesy Hank Gutman; page 66, boys eating, 1940, courtesy Camp Yawgoog; birthday party, courtesy Camp Bauercrest; page 67, empty dining hall, courtesy Camp Watitoh; page 69, title graphic, courtesy Camp Greylock for Boys; page 68, girls at rest hour, 1971, courtesy Camp Walden, photograph by Bob Duncan; page 69, boy writing letter, 1937, courtesy Camp Wigwam; haircut, circa 1959, courtesy Camp Wigwam; page 70, girl writing letter, courtesy Camp Walden; "Dear Pal, . . .", 1942, courtesy Nahum Waxman; **page 71,** the Coke machine, 1946, courtesy Camp Walden; **page 72,** boy reading comic, courtesy Camp Watitoh; Dennis the Menace® panel from "Dennis Goes to Camp" reprinted by courtesy of Hank Ketcham and © by Field Enterprises Inc.; **page 73,** opening package, 1954, courtesy Alford Lake Camp; boy with two packages, courtesy Camp Bauercrest; **page 75,** title graphic, courtesy *The Camping Magazine;* **page 74,** crafts room, 1935, courtesy Camp Walden; **page 75,** boy and puppet, courtesy Camp Wigwam; **page 76,** boy with model ship, courtesy Camp Wigwam; loom room, courtesy Camp Kehonka; **page 77,** totem pole and bookends, courtesy Dr. Eliot Berson; jewelry holder, circa 1958, courtesy I. Cyrus Gutman; snake head, courtesy Dr. Paul Rosenberg; **page 79,** title graphic, courtesy Camp Winnebago; **page 78,** the *J* stroke, courtesy Camp Kehonka; **page 79,** swamped canoe, Camp Lenore, 1954, courtesy Camp Lenore-Owaissa; emptying the canoe, Camp Lenore, 1954, courtesy Camp Lenore-Owaissa; **page 80,** war canoe aloft, courtesy Luther Gulick Camps; sail canoe, courtesy Camp Tapawingo; **page 81,** rigging the sails, 1956, courtesy Camp Winona; sunfish, Camp Hiawatha, courtesy Camp Wigwam; hiking out, courtesy Camp Kehonka, photograph by Roy Ballantine; **page 82,** fishing, courtesy Camp Mah-Kee-Nac; tilting, courtesy Alford Lake Camp; **page 83,** aquaplaning, courtesy Tripp Lake Camp; water ballet, courtesy Camp Kehonka; **page 85,** title graphic, courtesy Mutual Security Life; **page 84,** two girls, courtesy Tripp Lake Camp; **page 85,** buried alive, Camp Wigwam beach trip, 1959, authors' collection; **page 86,** group at signpost, courtesy Camp Wigwam; **page 87,** cog railway, 1946, courtesy Camp Wicosuta; girls around car, courtesy Alford Lake Camp; **page 88,** quarry, courtesy Camp Wigwam; **page 89,** big shoe, courtesy Camp Bauercrest; view from peak, 1924, courtesy Camp Wigwam; taking a swig, 1924, courtesy Camp Wigwam; **page 91,** title graphic, courtesy *The Camping Magazine;* page 90, boiling water test, courtesy Camp Kennebec; **page 91,** spit in the eye, Camp Somerset, 1939, courtesy Hildy Largman Stoumen; junior woodcraft lean-to, courtesy Camp Greylock for Boys; **page 92,** roasting a hot dog, courtesy Camp Kennebec; **page 93,** cleanup, courtesy Camp Unalayee; cookout, courtesy Camp Unalayee; **page 95,** title graphic, courtesy Schering-Plough Corporation; **page 94,** "Say, *aah,*" 1942, courtesy Camp Yawgoog; **page 95,** rest cottage, 1928, courtesy Camp

Lenox for Boys; **page 97,** title graphic, courtesy Camp Greylock for Boys; **page 96,** Runoia play, courtesy Camp Runoia; **page 97,** swordplay, courtesy Camp Wigwam; **page 98,** bunk shows, courtesy Camp Walden; *H.M.S. Pinafore,* 1937, courtesy Camp Greylock for Boys; **page 99,** all-camp production, courtesy The National Music Camp; girls' tableau, courtesy Camp Watitoh; **page 100,** camp band, courtesy Camp Pemigewassett; girls practicing, courtesy The National Music Camp; **page 101,** leopard dance, courtesy Tripp Lake Camp; dancer, Camp Somerset, 1937, courtesy Hildy Largman Stoumen; **page 103,** title graphic, courtesy Boy Scouts of America; **page 102,** canoe trailer, courtesy Camp Tapawingo; **page 103,** hiker with bucket, French Camp, 1919, authors' collection; **page 105,** pushing canoe, courtesy Camp Walden; cooking a meal, courtesy Camp Walden; sitting in the sand, courtesy Camp Walden; **page 106,** trippers on canoes, courtesy Camp Wigwam; **page 107,** Good morning! French Camp, 1919, authors' collection; cooking breakfast, French Camp, 1919, authors' collection; ready for the descent, French Camp, 1919, authors' collection; **page 108,** two backpackers, courtesy Camp Unalayee; **page 109,** fish from Lake Champlain, 1930, courtesy Camp Dudley; girls on trail, courtesy Camp Walden; **page 111,** title graphic, from *Camps and Camping,* Spalding's Athletic Library, 1924; **page 110,** bingo, courtesy Camp Bauercrest; **page 111,** rain gear, from *Camps and Camping,* Spalding's Athletic Library, 1924; storytelling, 1930, courtesy Camp Greylock for Boys; **page 113,** title graphic, courtesy Camp Greylock for Boys; **page 112,** goose float, courtesy Camp Kehonka; **page 113,** counselor dunk, courtesy Camp Wicosuta; **page 114,** eggs on spoons, courtesy Camp Lenox for Boys; rodeo, courtesy The Cheley Colorado Camps; **page 115,** canoe float, courtesy Camp Wigwam; circus, courtesy Camp Greylock for Boys; **page 117,** title graphic, courtesy General Foods Corp.; **page 116,** the gang, Camp Kennebec, circa 1954, courtesy Hildy Largman Stoumen; with dad, Camp Kennebec, circa 1954, courtesy Hildy Largman Stoumen; with mom, Camp Kennebec, circa 1954, courtesy Hildy Largman Stoumen; **page 119,** title graphic, *Camp Life* magazine; **page 118,** Bible story, Camp Lenore, courtesy Camp Lenore-Owaissa; **page 119,** altar, Camp Kehonka, photograph by R.J.S. Gutman, 1981; sign, Camp Takajo, photograph by R.J.S. Gutman, 1981; **page 121,** title graphic, *Camp Life* magazine; **page 120,** song leaders, courtesy Camp Chewonki, photograph by Bruce

McMillan; **page 121,** preparing for the campfire, courtesy Camp Lenox for Boys; **page 122,** small campfire group, 1946, courtesy Camp Pemigewassett; guitar and accordion, 1950, courtesy Camp Greylock for Boys; **page 123,** postcard home, 1948, courtesy Hank Gutman; chef's hat boxing, courtesy *The Camping Magazine,* June 1937; burnt marshmallow, circa 1971, courtesy Camp Lenox for Boys; **page 125,** title graphic, *Camping World* magazine; **page 124,** Mexican hat dance, courtesy Camp Runoia; **page 125,** masquerade, Camp Somerset, circa 1930, courtesy Mildred Largman Gutman; **page 126,** audience, courtesy Camp Wigwam; baggy jeans, courtesy Camp Wigwam; **page 127,** social, Camp Hiawatha, courtesy Camp Wigwam; **page 128,** musicale, courtesy Camp Kehonka, photograph by Ned Bullock; **page 129,** boxing, circa 1920, courtesy Camp Lenox for Boys; **page 130,** jacks, courtesy Camp Walden; pillow fight, courtesy Camp Wigwam; **page 131,** skinny dipper, Camp Fernwood, courtesy Jane Shapiro Baum; hidden bed, The Wyonegonic Camps, photograph by R.J.S. Gutman, 1981; **page 133,** title graphic, courtesy Camp Wigwam; **page 132,** seated girls, courtesy Forest Acres; **page 133,** cheerleader, Camp Wigwam, 1954, courtesy Norman Makransky; **page 134,** comic strip, *The Totem Pole,* Camp Wigwam, 1947, courtesy Kenneth Greif; **page 135,** hoop rolling, courtesy Camp Walden; under-the-leg relay, 1939, courtesy Camp Greylock for Boys; tug of war, 1931, courtesy Camp Greylock for Boys; **page 136,** anchor formation, Camp Hiawatha, 1961, courtesy Renie Kay Seff; **page 139,** title graphic, courtesy *The Camping Magazine;* **page 138,** boat tow, 1940, courtesy Luther Gulick Camps; **page 139,** flaming "80," 1980, courtesy Camp Androscoggin; **page 141,** Ideal Girl, courtesy Camp Waldemar; **page 143,** title graphic, courtesy Camp Greylock for Boys; **page 142,** suitcases, circa 1958, courtesy Camp Wigwam; **page 144,** comic strip. *The Totem Pole,* Camp Wigwam, 1961, courtesy Camp Wigwam; airing out the trunk, courtesy Camp Dudley; cub reporter, *The Totem Pole,* Camp Wigwam, 1951, courtesy Kenneth Greif; **page 145,** final campfire, 1941, courtesy Luther Gulick Camps; final banquet, Camp Hiawatha, courtesy Camp Wigwam; **page 146,** lake swim club award, Camp Takajo, photograph by R.J.S. Gutman, 1981; awaiting the train, courtesy Camp Dudley; **page 147,** So long, *Androscoggin Junior 1953* yearbook, courtesy Camp Androscoggin.